THE GOOD, THE BAD
and the WURST

THE GOOD, THE BAD
and the WURST

The 100 Craziest Moments from
the Eurovision Song Contest

GEOFF TIBBALLS

ROBINSON

ROBINSON

First published in Great Britain in 2016 by Robinson

A CIP catalogue record for this book
is available from the British Library.

ISBN 978-1-47213-706-7 (paperback)

Typeset in Nexus Serif by Hewer Text UK Ltd, Edinburgh
Printed and bound in Great Britain by Clays Ltd, Elcograf S.p.A.
Papers used by Robinson are from well-managed forests and other responsible sources

Robinson
is an imprint of
Little, Brown Book Group
Carmelite House
50 Victoria Embankment
London EC4Y 0DZ

An Hachette UK Company
www.hachette.co.uk

www.littlebrown.co.uk

CONTENTS

INTRODUCTION

For sixty years the Eurovision Song Contest has been one of life's guilty pleasures. Existing in a parallel universe where a song about the construction of a hydroelectric power station is considered cutting-edge pop, where half a dozen warbling Russian grandmothers are considered Saturday-night entertainment, where a tune repeating the word 'la' 138 times is considered a winner and where Australia is considered part of Europe, the Eurovision beguiles and bemuses 200 million viewers globally each year.

We watch the Eurovision as adults for much the same reason that as children we used to insist on touching a park bench with the sign 'Wet paint' hanging from it. We know we shouldn't but we just can't help ourselves. So we tune in faithfully year after year, but not in the hope of the standard ever improving. That ship sailed long ago. Back in 1982, France declined to enter, labelling the contest 'a monument to drivel'. The biggest surprise was that it had taken them twenty-six years to notice. How can an event that last produced a truly memorable song as long ago as 1974 give genuine cause for optimism?

We don't care because the Eurovision is about much more than the music (which, to be honest, is just as well) – it is a glittering, over-the-top extravaganza, a feast of lamé, latex and leather, an essential date in the calendar that appeals to the British love of the absurd. If it suddenly became even half-decent we would probably desert it in our droves. As Jeremy Paxman acidly remarked: 'It's Eurovision – time to send the brain away for the weekend.'

In the early days, the Eurovision was always delightfully out of step with reality. At the height of Beatlemania, from 1963 to 1966, the UK entries were Ronnie Carroll, Matt Monro, Kathy Kirby and Kenneth McKellar respectively – hardly reflective of the swinging sixties. From our annual dip into Europop we deduced that most of mainland Europe still appeared to be yodelling, whistling, and playing the accordion and, in turn, heaven knows what their viewers must have thought of our singers. In the case of Matt Monro the opinion probably had something to do with a desire to adjust the horizontal hold on the TV set, as his head always appeared to be disproportionately large in relation to the rest of his body.

Although we in the UK may once have sniggered about preposterous Austrian mullets and songs about lovesick Albanian shepherds, in recent years we have shown that when we really put our mind to it we can produce music as instantly forgettable as any other country in Europe. Our cause is not helped by a voting system – once considered quaint, with an air of helping out a neighbour in need – which now smacks of a vast conspiracy. Indeed controversy has regularly darkened the sparkly doors of the Eurovision.

Over sixty years we have witnessed scandals – including vote-rigging allegations – and we have witnessed national outrage on an annual basis, but most have all we have witnessed silly costumes, terrible lyrics, and performers as diverse as Celine Dion and Dustin the Turkey. This book chronicles the hundred craziest moments – the mad acts, the sad acts, the bad acts, the drag acts, and the *nul points* heroes.

Many words have been written about the Eurovision Song Contest. No doubt that great philosopher, Swiss Toni from *The Fast Show*, would have compared the Eurovision to having sex with a beautiful woman. It looks fantastic, makes a lot of noise, goes on for three hours, all the neighbours are watching, and at the end you get judged.

ACKNOWLEDGEMENTS

The author would like to thank the following lyricists for their contribution to the culture of the Eurovision Song Contest: Émile Gardaz ('Refrain'), Syd Cordell ('Sing Little Birdie'), Guy Favereau (*'Printemps, Avril Carillonne'*), Peter Warne ('Boom Bang-a-Bang'), Derry Lindsay and Jackie Smith ('All Kinds of Everything'), Lars Forssell ('You're Summer'), Bob Williams ('It's Just a Game'), Will Luikinga and Eddy Ouwens ('Ding Dinge Dong'), Michael Fotiades (*'Panagia Mou, Panagia Mou'*), Peter Reber ('Djambo, Djambo'), Vexi Salmi ('Pump-Pump'), Lukas Resetarits ('Boom Boom Boomerang'), Bernd Meinunger ('Dschinghis Khan'), Sofia Tsotou ('Sokrati'), Ragnar Olsen ('Sami Earth'), Juice Leskinen (*'Nuku Pommiin'*), Britt Lindeborg ('Diggi-Loo Diggi-Ley'), Zohar Laskov (*'Shir Habatlanim'*), Paul Curtis ('A Message to your Heart'), Fahrudin Pecikova and Edin Dervishalidović (*'Sva Bol Svijeta'*), Nina Morato (*'Je Suis Un Vrai Garçon'*), Mark Berry and Martina Siber ('One Step'), Alf Poier (*'Weil Der Mensch Zählt'*), Andrius Mamontovas and Victor Diawara ('We Are the Winners'), Andrew Hill, Russ Spencer, Paul Tarry and Morten Schjolin ('Flying the Flag (For You)'), Darren Smith and Simon Fine (*'Irelande Douze Pointe'*), Bibi Kvachadze ('We Don't Wanna Put In'), Olga Tuktaryova and Mary S. Applegate ('Party For Everybody'), Lukas Plöchl and Manuel Hoffelner (*'Woki mit deim Popo'*).

TRUSTING THE SWISS (1956)

The man to blame for the Eurovision Song Contest is French-man Marcel Bezençon. He had been impressed by the success of Italy's Sanremo music festival, which started in 1951 and thought that a similar but expanded contest would be the ideal way of fostering unity among the various nations of Europe. Little did he know that the event would often bring discord rather than harmony.

Organised by the newly formed European Broadcasting Union, of which Bezençon was the president, the first Eurovision Song Contest was staged in Lugano, Switzerland, on 24 May 1956. Only seven countries took part – the Netherlands, Switzerland, Belgium, Germany, France, Luxembourg and Italy. In the UK, the BBC declined to enter, preferring to concentrate on its own jingoistic *Festival of British Popular Songs*. Who needs Johnny Foreigner when you've got Dennis Lotis, even though he was born in South Africa?

This left the Eurovision short of numbers, so to pad it out each nation had two songs. Most countries sent two singers, but Switzerland's Lys Assia performed both her country's entries. This is rather like riding two horses in a race, but less challeng-ing physically. She hedged her bets. Her first song, '*Das Alte Karussel*', sung in German, was a jolly ditty about an old carousel and would pave the way for countless Eurovision songs about puppets, circuses and clowns. Her second, the French 'Refrain', was an altogether sadder offering, mourning to the sound of wailing violins 'the colour of rain, the regret of my twenty years, anger, sadness of no longer being a child'. History tells us that melancholy rarely finds favour with Eurovision juries but this was the first year so they knew no better.

The voting at that first Eurovision took place in secret and there is no record of who voted for who. Each country had just two votes and could vote for its own song. Luxembourg was so strapped for cash that not only did it emulate Switzerland by sending only one singer, Michèle Arnaud, to perform both of its songs, but it also decided against the expense of sending a jury to Switzerland. Instead, in an extraordinary exhibition of trust, Luxembourg instructed the Swiss to vote on its behalf. So perhaps it was no great surprise that when all the secret votes were added up, Switzerland was declared the winner with 'Refrain'. Apparently, no rats were smelled.

Lys Assia evidently found the Eurovision such an enriching experience that she returned for the next two years and even attempted to represent her country again in the 2013 final, aged 89.

IT FINISHED WITH A KISS (1957)

The 1957 contest was held in Frankfurt, West Germany, with the UK entering for the first time. Wearing a long gown, wholesome soprano Patricia Bredin trilled her way through 'All' in just under two minutes, no doubt leading to hilarious backstage exchanges with people asking: 'Is that "All"?' She was followed by Italy's Nunzio Gallo, whose offering ran for over five minutes, including a fifty-five-second guitar intro. After that, a rule was introduced restricting each song to a maximum of three minutes. Thankfully, this still applies today because Eurovision goes on long enough as it is. Any longer and the final juries would still be voting on Sunday morning.

Back to 1957 and Austria's Bob Martin, who from his name might have been expected to sing a song about dogs but instead performed an uplifting ode to his pony and was rewarded by being voted into last place. The comfortable winner turned out to be the Netherlands' Corry Brokken but the most memorable moment of the evening was provided by Denmark's Birthe Wilke and Gustav Winckler, the first to take advantage of a new rule allowing duos to perform at the contest. Performing '*Skibet Skal Sejle I Nat*' ('The Ship Must Sail Tonight'), he, dressed as a naval captain, then slipped a ring on to her finger before ending the song with a farewell kiss that went on for thirteen long seconds because the stage manager forgot to shout 'Cut!' Neither party held back, and at one point poor Birthe appeared desperate to come up for air.

The incident might have caused a furore with outraged viewers labelling it the Eurovision Snog Contest but for the fact that in those days Eurovision was primarily a radio event with relatively few people having access to a television set. So the most erotic thing they would have heard was the sound of suction which listeners probably attributed to the conductor adjusting his dentures. It remains the longest kiss ever to have taken place in Eurovision and a record only likely to be broken if Graham Norton bumps into a mirror.

ITALY'S WINGS ARE CLIPPED (1958)

At the 1958 Eurovision, one song was clearly head and shoulders above the rest. Italy's '*Volare*' ('To Fly') – or as it was titled in the contest, '*Nel Blu Dipinto di Blu*' ('The Blue Painted in Blue') – went on to become a worldwide hit for Dean Martin and others, selling over 22 million copies. It has been recorded by artists of the calibre of Frank Sinatra, Ella Fitzgerald, Luciano Pavarotti, Louis Armstrong and David Bowie, has won a Grammy award, and was named *Billboard's* song of the year for 1958. Naturally it came third in Eurovision.

The track was co-written and performed by Domenico Modugno, the first to sing on the night in the Dutch city of Hilversum. He had to do it all over again at the end because a technical hitch meant that he had been neither seen nor heard in some countries. Italy faced nine rivals but the UK was not among them, having gone off in a huff after finishing only seventh the previous year. Its place was taken by Sweden in the shape of jazz singer Alice Babs whose song, '*Lilla Stjärna*' ('Little Star'), opened in the finest Eurovision tradition with thirty-four seconds of 'la la la's. She performed the song wearing the Leksand regional costume – a demure skirt and apron. It was a long way from Agnetha and Anni-Frid.

In accordance with a new voting system introduced in 1957, every participating country provided ten jury members, each awarding one point to their favourite song. Nearly all of the songs on offer were about love, including Switzerland's Lys Assia this time singing in Italian about 'Giorgio', with whom she had apparently spent a romantic weekend in Lake Maggiore. As the lyrics contain references to polenta, risotto and espresso, it would seem they spent most of their weekend eating. She eventually finished second on twenty-four points, three adrift of France's André Claveau with a ballad *Dors, Mon Amour* ('Sleep, My Love'). As a sedative, it was second to none. Poor Modugno trailed in a distant third, polling just thirteen votes, with only West Germany and Belgium awarding him more than one point and Denmark and Luxembourg ignoring him altogether. He would not be the last to be baffled by the voting of Eurovision juries but, if nothing else, he could wave his royalty cheques in their faces.

SING LITTLE BIRDIE (1959)

In 1959, the UK rock 'n' roll movement was in full swing. The charts were awash with the vibrant sounds of Adam Faith, Cliff Richard and Marty Wilde, the nation's answers to Elvis, Buddy Holly and Jerry Lee Lewis. Rock ruled the airwaves. So on our return to the Eurovision fold, who did we send to that year's contest? Wholesome husband-and-wife team Teddy Johnson and Pearl Carr, the Terry and June of their day, with the relentlessly chirpy 'Sing, Little Birdie'. To rock fans, it was lip-curlingly awful.

Penned by Syd Cordell and Stan Butcher, 'Sing, Little Birdie' correlated the birds singing in the sky with Carr and Johnson's enduring love for each other. The chorus trilled: 'Sing, little birdie, sing your song, Sing, you'll help our love along.' It was joyous, it was nauseous, it was Eurovision.

Successful solo performers before marrying in 1955, Carr and Johnson were mainstays of many a forgettable TV light entertainment show, performing alongside tap dancers, jugglers, acrobats and people who did strange things with balloons. The duo were the penultimate performers on the night in Cannes following such gems as an Austrian song that combined calypso and yodelling, a Danish ditty with a xylophone riff, and a French number titled '*Oui, Oui, Oui, Oui*', which may have sounded orgasmic, but in reality was more of an anti-climax. The UK led the field at the halfway stage but ultimately even Johnson's whistling solo was not enough to fend off the challenge of the Dutch entry, '*Een Beetje*' ('A Little Bit') sung by another Teddy, Teddy Scholten (although this was a female Teddy, real name Dorothea). The UK finished second, leaving the French singer, Jean Philippe, in third, to cry '*Oui, Oui, Oui, Oui*' all the way home.

An innovation, never to be repeated again, saw not just the winner but the first three songs performed again at the end of the show, prompting viewers to wail in their droves: 'Mr Eurovision, you have delighted us long enough.'

'Sing, Little Birdie' achieved an afterlife of sorts as an ironic answer in the *Monty Python's Flying Circus* sketch 'World Forum', in which Mao Tse-tung buzzed in correctly to display his vast Eurovision knowledge and beat fellow quizzers Che Guevara, Vladimir Lenin and Karl Marx.

CALLING ALL REINDEER (1960)

Norway made its Eurovision debut in 1960 with what would turn out to be a typically idiosyncratic entry. 'Voi Voi' ('Hey Hey'), composed by Georg Elgaaen and sung by Nora Brockstedt, was an arrangement of a Lapp reindeer-herding call, not an obvious source of inspiration for a popular song contest. But, hey hey, this is Eurovision, which is pretty much a law unto itself.

Brockstedt was already an established artist in Norway, where she had enjoyed a succession of singalong hits and been one of six members of popular Scandinavian vocal group the Monn Keys. In hindsight, how tempting it must have been for her to introduce her Eurovision entry in English with the words 'Hey, hey, we're the Monn Keys.'

This was also the year when Caterina Irene Elena Maria Imperiali di Francavilla began her long association with the Eurovision Song Contest, presenting the show to the whole of Europe from London's Royal Festival Hall as the more recognisable Katie Boyle. The elegant daughter of an Italian marquis, she had been a BBC continuity announcer before blossoming into a personality in her own right. She would soon use her fame to promote Camay soap in a series of TV commercials with the jingle 'You'll look a little lovelier each day, with fabulous pink

Camay.' She lent an air of sophistication to Camay at a time when rival brand Lifebuoy preferred to focus on its ability to combat body odour. There was as much chance of Katie Boyle having sweaty armpits as there was of her presenting the contest wearing a pair of ripped jeans.

Representing the host country was Teddy Johnson's brother Bryan (definitely not to be confused with the Brian Johnson of AC/DC) singing 'Looking High, High, High', the sort of rousing tune one might imagine emanating from Boy Scout campfires. Like his brother, Bryan incorporated a spot of gratuitous whistling and also finished second, seven points behind winners France. The fact that Norway came a creditable fourth suggested that the Eurovision juries contained a disproportionately high number of reindeer herders.

BING ET BONG ET BING ET BONG (1961)

Picture the scene. Lyricist Guy Favereau is toiling away in his study trying to conjure up suitable words for France's prospective Eurovision entry. It is to be called '*Printemps, Avril Carillonne*' ('Springtime, April Rings'), which is fair enough as the contest was staged on 18 March that year. He has a nice chorus about the animals all coming out of hibernation in readiness for the warmer weather. What he needs now is an opening line for each verse that will match Francis Baxter's lively tune. Then, in a Eureka moment, it comes to him: he will start the verses with 'Bing et bong et bing et bong'. Genius, and if anyone should ask him what it means he can reply with the familiar Gallic shrug. Little did he know that in that moment he was setting the gold standard for future Eurovision lyricists which states that if you can't think of anything, just lob in a few meaningless bings and bongs. The juries will love it. Academics refer to it as the 'Bing tiddle-tiddle bong' phenomenon.

For the first time, the Eurovision, staged again in Cannes, took place on a Saturday night, where it has resolutely remained ever since, spoiling many an otherwise pleasant weekend.

As well as the French entry, performed by Jean-Paul Mauric, several other countries offered songs about the seasons. Monaco sung about happiness on a spring day, Sweden's was titled 'April, April', Nora Brockstedt returned for Norway to sing about summer in Palma, while Belgium's Bob Benny was a little out of step calendar-wise with '*September, Gouden Roos*' ('September, Golden Rose'). Maybe he had overslept. Elsewhere, Franca di Rienzo performed for Switzerland wearing a daring strapless gown that helped her to third place, just ahead of France's bings and bongs.

One place ahead of her, finishing second for the third successive year, was the UK entry. Where the Allisons' 'Are You Sure?' differed from its two UK predecessors was that it actually sounded like a contemporary pop song as opposed to something that was at least twenty-five years past its sell-by date. The Allisons were a cut-price Everly Brothers, although they weren't actually brothers at all, John Alford and Bob Day taking their name from Alford's schoolgirl sweetheart, Allison. 'Are You Sure?' went on to sell over a million records but the duo were unable to follow up its success and disbanded just two years later to be consigned to the ranks of one-hit wonders. In truth, the song was probably too good for Eurovision, trailing seven points behind the winner, Luxembourg's Jean-Claude Pascal with '*Nous Les Amoureux*' ('We, The Lovers'). Perhaps in a fit of pique about finishing second again, the BBC failed to repeat the winning song at the end of the broadcast on the grounds that the contest had overrun. There were few complaints.

PLUNGED INTO DARKNESS (1962)

The eighteenth of March 1962 wasn't quite the night the lamps went out all over Europe but a series of power cuts and technical glitches disrupted that year's Eurovision, leaving the Dutch feeling particularly hard done by. The stage in the grand auditorium of the Villa Louvigny in Luxembourg was decorated with twinkling stars but problems with the lighting frequently blacked them out altogether. Immediately after the French entry, the picture from Luxembourg was lost, only to be restored a couple of minutes later, to the dismay of millions.

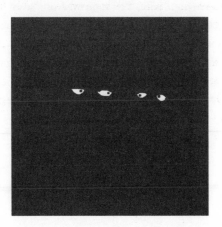

However, the greatest misfortune befell Dutch male singing duo De Spelbrekers whose performance of 'Katinka' was seen largely in negative as the gremlins struck again to plunge the screen into semi-darkness. The pair were wild-eyed at the best of times, but in negative they looked like a couple of gravediggers from a Boris Karloff horror film. The fault did them no favours and with another new voting system in place (for one year only), they were one of four nations to finish with *nul points*. Keeping them company was Fud Leclerc, making his fourth spectacularly unsuccessful appearance in the contest for Belgium. Realising that the voters of Europe might be trying to tell him something, he decided that it should also be his last appearance.

France won for the third time with a song about first love while, after the brief hint at modernity provided by the Allisons, the UK sadly reverted to type with Belfast plumber's son Ronnie Carroll performing 'Ring-a-Ding Girl', a song every bit as dire as its title suggests. Inspired no doubt by the French bings and bongs of the previous year, it repeated the line 'ring-ding-a-ding-a-ding, ding-ding' throughout its three long minutes. Tinnitus would have been preferable. That it finished as high as fourth tells you pretty much all you need to know about the Eurovision Song Contest.

WHISTLING IN THE CANTEEN (1962)

One song that didn't make it to the 1962 Eurovision was '*Jeg Snakker Med Mig Selv*' ('I Talk To Myself'), a swing-style number performed by Gitte Hænning. It was one of six songs lined up for that year's Dansk Melodi Grand Prix (the Danish national selection contest), only to be disqualified before the event after its composer, Sejr Volmer-Sørensen, was heard whistling the catchy tune in the canteen of Danish broadcaster DR. Bizarrely, this was deemed to have broken a competition rule stating that all songs must not previously have been performed in public.

Instead the Danes sent '*Vuggevise*' ('Lullaby', performed by Ellen Winther) to Luxembourg, where it picked up a miserable two points – and no surprise that one of those came from Sweden. Hænning did eventually get her shot at Eurovision glory eleven years later when she represented Germany as Gitte, but finished only eighth with '*Junger Tag*' ('Young Day'). In 1978, she tried to represent a third country, Luxembourg, but lost out to Spanish female duo Baccara of 'Yes, Sir, I Can Boogie' infamy. When you lose to Baccara, you know it's time to call it a day.

HELLO, LONDON,
THIS IS OSLO . . . (1963)

**Transmitted from BBC Television Centre in London, the 1963
Eurovision line-up included nineteen-year-old French pop star
and future fashion icon Françoise Hardy singing for Monaco,
Greece's Nana Mouskouri performing for Luxembourg, and
Israeli singer Esther Ofarim – who, five years later with hubby
Abi would enjoy a UK No. 1 with the novelty hit 'Cinderella
Rockefella' – representing Switzerland.**

The voting juries, still firmly stuck in the 1950s, clearly felt
Hardy was way too modern for their tastes and placed her
self-composed *'L'Amour S'En Va'* ('Love Goes Away') only fifth. To
add insult to injury she even finished behind Ronnie Carroll,
representing the UK for the second successive year, presumably
in the belief that there is no substitute for blandness. Mlle Hardy
was probably philosophical about the result and doubtless realised that even if Elvis had pitched up to represent Finland in 1963
he would have been hard-pressed to get more than a handful of
votes from the other European juries.

As the voting progressed, the contest developed into a straight
fight between two songs – Denmark's *'Dansevise'* ('Dance Song'),
performed by Grethe and Jørgen Ingmann, and Esther Ofarim's

'*T'En Va Pas*' ('Don't Go Away') for Switzerland. After four of the sixteen rounds, Switzerland was one point ahead of Denmark. Next it was Norway's turn to vote but the spokesman in Oslo did not follow the correct procedure.

The song number, followed by the country, should have been announced before awarding the points. Even so, viewers at home could clearly understand that the Norwegian jury awarded a maximum five points to the UK, four to Italy, three to Switzerland, two to Denmark and one to Germany and those votes were correctly added to the scoreboard. But presenter Katie Boyle, anxious to make sure that everything was in order, asked Norway to repeat the votes. The jury spokesman had already sounded somewhat hesitant and this request seemed to confuse him completely so he instead suggested that London should go back to him after everyone else had cast their votes.

In the meantime, the remaining nations voted and after the last scheduled jury, Luxembourg, had given its votes, Switzerland was the winner on 42 points – two ahead of Denmark. Or so everyone thought. For it was then time to return to Oslo for confirmation of the votes of the Norwegian jury. Except this time, they were different. Norway still awarded five points to the UK, but this time gave four to Denmark, three to Italy, two to Germany and only one to Switzerland. This meant adding two points to the Danish total and subtracting two from the Swiss, thus reversing the result and making Denmark – Norway's Scandinavian neighbour – the unexpected winner.

The shock result brought audible mutterings of disquiet from the London audience, and the normally unflappable Boyle appeared understandably perplexed, especially as she then had to get back on the phone to the Monaco jury who had managed to award one vote too many. Monaco's miscalculation did not affect the two leading protagonists and Denmark was declared the controversial victor.

Naturally, questions were asked, but a European Broadcasting Union investigation exonerated Norway of any skulduggery. The explanation was that the jury spokesman had not been ready when London came to him first time around and, in a blind panic, had read out the wrong scores. And that, m'lud, is the case for the defence . . .

ON YER BIKE! (1963)

The interval act is a key element in the Eurovision Song Contest, an opportunity for viewers to take a deep breath and recover from the heady entertainment set before them. Thirty-one years before *Riverdance* pranced onto our screens, the BBC's idea of an interval diversion was five minutes of cycling, courtesy of Swedish speciality act Ola and Barbro. Round and round the stage they pedalled – balancing, swivelling, performing handstands, riding backwards and cycling on one wheel – her sometimes perched on his shoulders – and all to the gentle accompaniment of orchestral music. If nothing else, they had obviously passed the Swedish equivalent of the cycling proficiency test. The only disappointment was that Katie Boyle did not attach a pair of cycle clips to her ball gown and join in the merriment.

POLITICAL PROTEST (1964)

As a live event broadcast to many countries, Eurovision, for all its apparent innocence and irrelevance, would always be a target for those wishing to score political points. So it proved in Copenhagen in 1964 immediately after the Swiss performance, when a lone protester climbed on the stage with a banner saying 'Boycott Franco and Salazar' in reference to the right-wing dictatorships in Spain and Portugal respectively. While the gentleman was escorted out, TV viewers were shown a prolonged shot of the scoreboard which made for riveting viewing as it was still blank because nobody had voted yet.

Another new voting system was introduced, for the third consecutive year, with each nation awarding five points, three points and one point to its three favourite songs. Sweden declined to enter, citing a strike by its musicians' union and insisting that the withdrawal was in no way connected to the *nul points* it had scored the previous year. Portugal took Sweden's place among the sixteen nations but its debut, perhaps influenced by the protest, resulted in the dreaded total of zero. Spain, the other targeted country, fared little better in accruing just one point, its cause not helped by the fact that performers Nelly, Tim and Tony owed more to Rod, Jane and Freddy than to Peter, Paul and Mary. Apart from Portugal, three other countries scored *nul points* – Yugoslavia, Switzerland and Germany, although it was hard to see how the last named could fail with a title as catchy as '*Man Gewöhnt Sich so Schnell an das Schöne*' ('How Quickly We Get Used to Nice Things').

Italy's Gigliola Cinquetti was the runaway winner, scoring nearly three times as many points as her closest rival, the UK's Matt Monro, who finished runner-up with the Tony Hatch composition 'I Love the Little Things'. It was not an entirely wasted evening for Monro, however. He liked the sixth-placed Austrian song so much that he recorded it an English as 'Walk Away' and enjoyed a hit on both sides of the Atlantic. By contrast, 'I Love the Little Things' sank without trace.

KICKING AND SCREAMING (1965)

Bedfellows don't come much more unlikely than Serge Gainsbourg and the Eurovision Song Contest. The Frenchman who, three years later, would perform the erotic duet *'Je t'Aime . . . Moi Non Plus'* with Jane Birkin, was not someone that you would readily associate with a contest that popularised songs about windmills and flowers. However, he was persuaded to write an entry for his seventeen-year-old god-daughter France Gall, although to the annoyance of the French press and public, *'Poupée de Cire, Poupée de Son'* ('Wax Doll, Rag Doll') represented Luxembourg rather than the home country of both composer and performer. That resentment turned to downright anger when the gamine Gall emerged victorious on the night in Naples, beating France into third place.

Set against the usual array of more mature performers trotting out traditional Eurovision fodder, the trendy young Gall singing an up-to-the-minute song is widely seen as the moment when the contest was finally dragged kicking and screaming into the 1960s. It was the first non-ballad to win, yet it was by no means a smooth ride. During rehearsals, there were said to be mutterings of discontent about a song that strayed so far from the Eurovision norm, and when Gall called her lover at the time, singer Claude

François, immediately after the performance, he shouted at her: 'You sang off-key! You were terrible!' That may sound harsh but, to be fair to him, he had yet to hear Jemini.

Meanwhile, during its year of absence, Sweden had come up with a cunning plan. Instead of singing in a language unintelligible to most of Europe, it would perform in English. Even though Ingvar Wixell's 'Absent Friend' finished only tenth, the incident unnerved contest bosses to the extent that a new rule was introduced stipulating that in future all songs should be performed in the native tongue. The rule lasted until 1973, and was relaxed just in time for ABBA.

BEYOND OUR KEN (1966)

Following the triumph of France Gall, most of the entrants for the 1966 contest decided that what was now needed was a pretty girl singing a bouncy song. The line-up included several of that ilk, including Norway's Åse Kleveland – who, in wearing a trouser suit, became the first woman at Eurovision not to perform in a dress. She would later become her country's minister of culture, which just shows what can happen when you dare to be different.

Also bucking the trend – but in the wrong way – was the UK, which selected as its representative 38-year-old Scottish tenor Kenneth McKellar, stalwart of *The White Heather Club* and many a Hogmanay production. To say he appealed to an older audience was an understatement. Whereas Tom Jones's fans hurled their knickers onstage, McKellar's were more likely to lob their orthopaedic stockings. Perhaps in the hope of being mistaken for a young girl in a skirt by short-sighted jurors, McKellar decided at the last minute to change into a kilt to perform his song 'A Man Without Love'. When he walked onstage at Luxembourg's grand auditorium, there were audible gasps from the audience who, unfamiliar with the Scottish national costume, must have feared they were about to witness Eurovision's first cross-dresser.

Although, mercifully, he made no attempt to pre-empt Bucks Fizz by whipping the garment off mid-song, the kilt did not prove a vote-winner. For despite singing last on the night – often seen as an advantage in a contest largely composed of the quickly forget-table – he finished a distant ninth, which at the time was the UK's worst result.

A HISSY FIT (1966)

Making his third Eurovision appearance, Italy's Domenico Modugno blew a fuse during dress rehearsals and stormed off because he was unhappy with the orchestra. There was some doubt as to whether he would return for the actual contest, but he eventually backed down and performed '*Dio, Come Ti Amo*' ('God, How I Love You') with such emotion that he appeared to be on the verge of tears – a sentiment shared by many viewers, although not necessarily for the same reason. His song was a dramatic ballad with a curious instrumental arrangement that seemed to be for a different song, and it baffled the voting juries so much that they totally ignored it, putting it joint last (with Monaco) on *nul points*. He must have wished he had gone home after all.

THE RELUCTANT HEROINE (1967)

As Britain's barefoot pop princess with a string of hits already to her name, pretty much the last thing Sandie Shaw wanted to do in 1967 was sing at Eurovision. She was a glamorous sixties' icon, the original Essex girl made good (she once worked in the Ford factory at Dagenham) and, not unreasonably, she thought that a contest widely viewed as a celebration of the inconsequential might damage her credibility. It was like asking Bob Dylan to do summer season in Blackpool. However, Shaw's formidable manager Eve Taylor had other ideas and persuaded her to take part as a step towards moving onto the lucrative cabaret circuit. Even so, the singer's participation was thrown into doubt when she was involved in a divorce scandal involving a TV executive, and the BBC almost withdrew her from the contest for fear of a public backlash against her behaviour.

Shaw was given five songs to sing on *The Rolf Harris Show*. Of the five, she liked 'Puppet on a String' by Phil Coulter and Bill Martin least of all. She later said, 'I hated it from the very first "oompah" to the final bang on the big bass drum. Even in those days, before the phrase "chauvinist pig" had been coined, I was instinctively repelled by its sexist drool and cuckoo-clock tune.' She was therefore dismayed when it was chosen to go forward to the contest in Vienna.

Despite her misgivings, she performed the song on the night with tremendous verve, even overcoming a faulty microphone, which cut out right at the start. It has since been claimed that Eve Taylor deliberately sabotaged the microphone in a bid to win sympathy for the UK song. Shaw did not need the sympathy vote and won easily, overcoming, among others, an early example of Eurovision political correctness in Portugal's colonial policy appraisal '*O Vento Mudou*' ('The Wind has Changed'), Monaco's 'Boum Badaboum' (sung by young Minouche Barelli when it was so obviously tailor-made for Basil Brush) and '*L'Amour est Bleu*' ('Love is Blue'), performed by Vicky Leandros for Luxembourg as plain Vicky. The last-named song finished only fourth but would go on to be an international bestseller.

Shaw was so exhausted by the event and the unpleasantness surrounding the scandal that she didn't feel much like celebrating her win. Locked out of her hotel room, she fell asleep in the corridor in her fur coat clutching a bottle of champagne.

The passage of time has not made her any more amenable towards the song, a stance which, unsurprisingly, has angered the writers. 'She's knocked "Puppet" since she sang it,' said Bill Martin in 2015. 'She hadn't had a hit for several records prior to that and "Puppet" gave her a No. 1 all over the world. Yet she says it ruined her career. She was lucky to get it. I always want to tell her to give me the money back.'

FIXED BY FRANCO? (1968)

Following hot on the heels (not that Sandie Shaw was wearing any) of 'Puppet on a String', the UK realised that the way to win Eurovision was to unleash our biggest pop guns – and they didn't come any bigger than Cliff Richard. He may no longer have been the teen idol with the smouldering curled lip who once prompted newspapers to attack his 'crude exhibitionism' and to warn parents not to allow their daughters to go out with such people, but he was still the nation's favourite male solo artist – Mr Light Entertainment. Furthermore, Phil Coulter and Bill Martin, who wrote 'Puppet', had come up with another jaunty, upbeat number, 'Congratulations'. It had Eurovision success written all over it but nevertheless was not a bad song.

The show was staged at London's Royal Albert Hall and for the first time it was broadcast in colour, affording viewers at home the opportunity to appreciate fully the various hues of velour and satin. Sales of paracetamol probably doubled the next day. Cliff dressed for the occasion with a ruffled shirt that screamed Austin Powers. However, his performance could not be faulted. It received an ecstatic ovation and with only five songs remaining, the prize seemed in the bag.

Performing fifteenth out of the seventeen contestants was Spain's María Félix de los Ángeles Santamaría Espinosa, more conveniently known as Massiel. Her song, 'La La La', defined the term 'singalong' as it contained no fewer than 138 la's. As such, it transcended all language barriers, making it understood, if not appreciated, all the way from Finland to Yugoslavia. Massiel was not even originally scheduled to sing 'La La La'. That dubious honour was to have gone to Joan Manuel Serrat, but he insisted on performing it in Catalan, much to the annoyance of Spain's fascist dictator General Franco. As a result he was dropped from the competition. It is hard to imagine that 138 la's would sound much different in Catalan than in Spanish.

Unencumbered by any subtle nuances in the song, Massiel gave it her all but the result still seemed foregone. Sure enough, when it came to the voting, Cliff and 'Congratulations' forged ahead and, with two rounds to go, held a healthy three-point lead over Spain. Then Germany, perhaps in retaliation for the 1966 World Cup, awarded six votes to Spain and only two to the UK. The final jury, Yugoslavia, proceeded to ignore both songs, leaving Spain the winners by one point. Cliff was as ruffled as his shirt.

He had locked himself in the toilet during the voting because he wanted to avoid pretending to be happy for the cameras if he was losing. It proved a wise decision. An entire vineyard of sour grapes poured forth from Cliff fans, who suggested that the result was, at the very least, a travesty of justice but the singer himself maintained a dignified silence on the matter.

That is until 2008 when a Spanish documentary alleged what many had suspected all along – that the result was fixed. The film-makers claimed Franco was so desperate to improve Spain's international image that in the run-up to the 1968 contest he despatched corrupt Spanish TV executives around Europe to buy votes. The film's director, Montse Fernandez Vila, said that these executives 'travelled around Europe buying series that would never be broadcast and signing concert contracts with odd, unknown groups and singers. These contracts were translated into votes.'

Cliff was delighted at the prospect of the result being over-turned because 'it's never good to feel a loser. I've lived with this No. 2 thing for many years.' Yes, constipation can be a terrible problem.

Yet celebrations proved premature because the original result still stands, with seasoned Eurovision observers noting that Massiel's win might not necessarily have been down to vote-buying but could have been attributable to the fact that she sang the song on a popular German TV show the week before the contest. It was not even the last we had heard of the wretched song. She had the nerve to re-release it in 1997 with a hip-hop beat. It was slightly less irritating than the original but a minute longer, giving scope for even more la's. By my estimation – and I lost the will to live around 175 – there are close to two hundred la's in the remix. You have been warned.

WHERE ARE THE BOOM-BOOMS, ELTON? (1969)

Lulu drew the short straw in 1969. She performed six numbers on *A Song for Europe*, the traditional UK selection process, including 'I Can't Go On Living Without You' by the fledgling partnership of Elton John and Bernie Taupin. Naturally, this was overlooked in the public postcard vote (it was voted sixth out of six) with victory going to 'Boom Bang-A-Bang', a quintessential Eurovision offering with more booms and bangs than are healthy in one song. For their part, Elton and Bernie preferred to use proper words, which probably explains why, for all their success, they have never yet managed to crack the Eurovision Song Contest.

Written by Alan Moorhouse and Peter Warne, 'Boom Bang-A-Bang' is essentially a plea from the singer to her lover to give her a cuddle because 'My heart goes boom bang-a-bang, boom bang-a-bang when you are near, boom bang-a-bang, boom bang-a-bang loud in my ear.' And so on. A decent physician might have diagnosed cardiac arrhythmia, but Lulu was convinced that the condition was nothing to worry about.

The Eurovision-friendly lyrics, lively tune and Lulu's popularity all ensured that the song was well received in Madrid but it failed to stand out in a field of mediocrity and ended up tying for first place with three other countries: Spain, the Netherlands and France. The worst thing about the four-way tie was that it meant all four winning songs had to be reprised at the end of the show, which was more than many in the Teatro Real or at home could bear. In a bid to make sure that such a catastrophe was never repeated, the organisers resolved to change the voting system yet again.

In 1991, 'Boom Bang-A-Bang' was included on a blacklist of banned songs issued by the ever-cautious BBC during the first Gulf war. This was an eminently sensible decision since the troops on the front line were suffering enough already.

MARY, MARY, QUITE ORDINARY (1970)

Welsh folk singer Mary Hopkin was blessed with two benefactors whose names are rarely mentioned in the same sentence: Hughie Green and Paul McCartney. She first shot to fame on Green's *Opportunity Knocks*, the long-running talent show that brought us great acts like Les Dawson and Frank Carson but also, to balance things out, Lena Zavaroni, Neil Reid, Bobby Crush and Millican and Nesbitt the singing miners. For true aficionados, it also paraded the dubious talents of Gladys Brocklehurst, a buxom Lancashire mill girl who, while singing, used to grab husband Norman by the hair and slap him. Then there was MP Barbara Castle's sixty-three-year-old housekeeper Mildred Bracey, who combined playing the piano with a voice that would have frightened King Kong.

Ah, those were the days, which, by pure coincidence, happened to be the title of Hopkin's first hit, produced by McCartney and released on the Beatles' Apple record label in 1968. With successful follow-ups under her belt, the unthreatening nineteen-year-old seemed a natural to represent the UK at the 1970 Eurovision in Amsterdam with 'Knock, Knock, Who's There?', a number so lightweight it was in danger of floating back to Britain. The UK delegation's confidence was such that an after-show victory party for Hopkin was planned in advance.

Alas, they had reckoned without Dana, an eighteen-year-old singer from Ireland. She was even younger than Hopkin, had an equally pure voice, looked just as innocent but importantly had a better song. Composed by two Dublin print workers, Derry Lindsay and Jackie Smith, 'All Kinds of Everything' listed some of the things that reminded the singer of her boyfriend – including 'Snowdrops and daffodils, butterflies and bees ... summertime, wintertime, spring and autumn, too ... budding trees, autumn leaves, a snowflake or two.' Basically, pretty much everything reminded her of him. She was dangerously obsessed. She probably had to be served with a restraining order a couple of months later. Had the song not been restricted to three minutes, no doubt she could have added other things that reminded her of him, but it's hard to find words that rhyme with 'dog breath' and 'flatulence'.

Dana faced only eleven rivals on the night. Norway and Sweden brought sick notes from their mums, Finland was feeling a bit tired and Portugal was washing its hair. Spain, however, was represented by Julio Iglesias, wearing an electric-blue suit and backed by three singers in bright pink. His song finished fourth, subject to an investigation by the fashion police.

'All Kinds of Everything' was never likely to be covered by Motörhead or Megadeth, but it proved too strong for the other songs, beating Hopkin into second place by six points. Dana was so shocked at winning that she had to be pushed physically on to the stage to receive her prize. While the UK delegation found that the only item to eat at their victory party was humble pie, Hopkin was generous in praise of her conqueror and, with echoes of Sandie Shaw, admitted that she found the whole experience humiliating. 'I was so embarrassed about it,' she said later. 'Standing on stage singing a song you hate is awful.' Almost as bad as for us at home having to listen to it.

WITH BORROWED CAMERAS (1971)

It was not only Dana who was surprised by her 1970 triumph; the cash-strapped Irish broadcaster RTE seemed to be caught on the hop, too. When, as is required of the winning nation, it staged the following year's event from the compact Gaiety theatre in Dublin, it was only RTE's second outside broadcast in colour – and even that was only achieved by borrowing colour cameras from the BBC.

What the 1971 contest lacked in funding, it made up for in charm with an interval display by the Bunratty Castle Entertainers. For six minutes, Eurovision viewers were treated to big hair, harps and fiddles plus a first glimpse of the Irish folk dancing that would be the highlight of the contest two decades later. They also saw bread being baked over an open fire and a man sneezing. What more could you ask for from interval entertainment?

By way of a change, yet another new voting structure was introduced for 1971 whereby each nation had just two jurors, one over the age of twenty-five and one under. There was no stipulation that they had to be interested in music (where Eurovision is concerned it would probably be a hindrance anyway), the sole requirement being that they were free to travel to Dublin on the first weekend in April.

With the contest set against the backdrop of the Troubles, the BBC feared a hostile reaction from the Dublin audience towards the UK and so selected Northern Irish singer Clodagh Rodgers as its representative. Nevertheless she still received death threats from the IRA. Her song 'Jack in the Box', an unsubtle replica of 'Puppet on a String', finished fourth – thirty points behind Monaco's Séverine who sang about 'A Bench, A Tree, A Street' ('*Un Banc, Un Arbre, Une Rue*'), which sounded like an ambitious Tommy Cooper magic trick.

Elsewhere, Luxembourg's entry consisted of singing 'Pomme, pomme, pomme' over and over again in a clear bid to win the fruit vote, and Belgium was forced to make a last-minute change after Nicole of Nicole and Hugo was suddenly taken ill with jaundice. They were replaced by Jacques Raymond and Lily Castel, but their song '*Goeiemorgen, Morgen*' ('Good Morning, Morning') finished only fourteenth. Not to be denied his shot at stardom, Hugo returned two years later with a fully recovered Nicole to represent Belgium at the 1973 contest. Dressed in purple, flared jumpsuits which made Hugo, with his distinctive hairstyle, look alarmingly like a glam rock vampire, they finished last with 'Baby Baby'.

YOUR BREASTS ARE LIKE
SWALLOWS A-NESTLING (1973)

In 1971, a new Eurovision rule allowed up to six performers on stage, thereby doing away with the old restrictions that limited acts to solo artists and duos. Under the old rules, the UK could only have been represented by the Dave Clark Two while our 1978 entry, five-piece band Co-Co, would have needed to be reduced to Co. Another contest rule for which we should be grateful is the one which banned live animals from the stage. These regulations have undoubtedly spared us endless children's choirs and loveable Latvians singing to puppies and kittens. Having said that, the presence on stage of a hungry lion would have been welcome at many a Eurovision.

Sweden's offering in Luxembourg for 1973 was 'You're Summer' by Nova and the Dolls. Originally called Malta, male singing duo Claes af Geijerstam and Göran Fristorp had to change their name to Nova to avoid confusion with the country, even though it was not competing that year. The Dolls were their three backing singers. The song compared a lover to summer, with the chorus featuring the memorable line, 'I am blue and I long for your caress. Oh, your breasts are like swallows a-nestling.' This was repeated twice more in case listeners couldn't quite believe what they had heard the first time. The tune, which had the distinction of being the first at any Eurovision to be conducted by a woman, Monica Dominique, was by no means the worst and finished a respectable fifth.

For Norway, the two-boy, two-girl Bendik Singers performed 'It's Just a Game' to a big band sound. Unfortunately the trumpets did not quite manage to drown out the contrived rhyme, 'Come on and join us, it's a game of girl-and-boyness.' This was one of the few English lines in the song which at various points lapsed into several other European languages in a shameless attempt to plunder votes. The ploy worked to a degree as Norway finished seventh, its highest placing for seven years. As a result, there was a suggestion that its 1974 entry might be sung in Klingon to appeal to the legions of *Star Trek* fans. Rather like a bad smell, the Bendik Singers hung around Eurovision for four years in all, with various members representing Norway as solo artists in 1974, 1975 and 1976.

DON'T SHOOT ME, I'M ONLY THE PIANO PLAYER (1973)

In the wake of the atrocity at the 1972 Munich Olympics, where eleven Israeli team members were killed by Palestinian terrorists, tensions ran high at the 1973 Eurovision Song Contest, in which Israel was participating for the first time. Before the contest, the floor manager at Luxembourg's Nouveau Théâtre warned members of the studio audience not to stand up when they applauded because they risked being shot by security forces. Fortunately, this being Eurovision, there was more likely to be a fire drill than a standing ovation.

IRISH EYES WEREN'T SMILING (1973)

Bouncing back from his 1968 disappointment, Cliff Richard was the UK representative in 1973 with 'Power to All Our Friends', but this time he could only finish third. Somewhat ungraciously he described the winning song from Luxembourg as 'dull', although he did concede that Anne-Marie David sang it sweetly. Still, Cliff fared better than José Carlos Ary dos Santos, the lyricist of Portugal's entry *'Tourada'* ('Bullfight'), who was jailed briefly because the song was thought to be critical of the country's authoritarian regime. 'We're going to grab the world by the horns of misfortune,' sang Fernando Tordo on his way to joint tenth place.

He shared that finishing position with twenty-three-year-old Irish singer Maxi, erstwhile member (along with Barbara Dixon and Adele King) of girl band Maxi, Dick and Twink. During rehearsals for Eurovision, Maxi (real name Irene McCoubrey) had a major falling-out with the Irish delegation over the arrangement of her song, 'Do I Dream'. At one point she refused to carry on and threatened to quit the show altogether, prompting a panicking RTE to send over a possible replacement singer, Tina Reynolds, who had to rehearse the song on the flight out to Luxembourg (although not, of course, during the safety demonstration). In the event she was not needed as Maxi went ahead and performed on the night. Happily, Reynolds' efforts were not entirely in vain because she went on to represent Ireland the following year, where she did better than Maxi, finishing seventh.

WHAT KATIE DID NEXT (1974)

The thought of Katie Boyle going commando on live TV seemed about as likely as Thora Hird swearing like a trooper during *Songs of Praise* **or Basil Brush joining the north Somerset hunt.** Yet that is precisely what happened in 1974 at the Eurovision Song Contest, which Boyle was hosting for the fourth time. It was staged at the Dome, Brighton, where the set lighting was so strong that Boyle's underwear was clearly visible beneath her too-tight, salmon-pink satin dress.

Moments before the broadcast began, the producer ran up to her and said, 'I'm sorry, but your underwear is showing through your dress. You're going to have to take it off.' At which point, a couple of burly stage hands put their hands up her dress and removed her bra and knickers with as much decorum as was possible in the circumstances. To cover her predicament, she carried her prompt cards positioned awkwardly low, well below her waist. But as the Dutch act featured a barrel organ and puppets, the sight of a lady's underwear – an aristocratic lady at that – was deemed unsuitable for children's entertainers. After all, you'd never see Sooty pawing Elle Macpherson.

ITALY SAYS, 'NO' (1974)

Italy refused to broadcast the 1974 contest live because it objected to its own song. Its entry '*Sì*' ('Yes'), sung by Gigliola Cinquetti, describes the singer's love for a man and her exhilaration when she finally says, 'Yes,' to him but state television channel RAI was concerned that, with the word '*sì*' repeated sixteen times in the song, it could be seen as subliminal support for a 'Yes' vote in the country's upcoming referendum on divorce. So it refused to screen the contest until after the referendum and the song remained censored on most Italian state TV and radio stations for more than a month. Consequently, even though it finished second in Brighton and became a big hit in the UK under the title 'Go', it failed to make the Top 40 chart in Italy.

The year 1974 belonged, of course, to ABBA. Their success with 'Waterloo' was helped in no small part by conductor Sven-Olof Walldoff taking to the rostrum dressed as Napoleon. In previous Eurovisions, the conductors had all looked like bank managers but Walldoff really entered into the spirit of the occasion. The victory was magnificent consolation for ABBA who had submitted 'Ring Ring' as a possible entry for the 1973 contest, only to see it beaten in the Swedish national competition by those breasts like swallows a-nestling.

THE CARNATION REVOLUTION (1974)

Lest you are ever tempted to dismiss the Eurovision as irrelevant and lightweight, consider this: in 1974, plotters behind the Portuguese military coup known as the Carnation Revolution used the radio play of the country's Eurovision entry, 'E Depois do Adeus' ('And After the Farewell') by Paulo de Carvalho as the signal for the tanks to move in on the streets of Lisbon. Toppling a government was something the Sex Pistols could only dream of.

The coup was a means of overthrowing dictator Marcello Caetano (who had succeeded António de Oliveira Salazar in 1968) and was staged by the left-wing Armed Forces Movement (MFA). The group of military officers opposed the long-standing regime, the Estado Novo. For some reason, they decided that the secret signal for the start of the coup should be the country's Eurovision entry, which eighteen days earlier in Brighton had finished joint last with Switzerland, Germany and Norway, having amassed only three points. It would be safe to say that ABBA did not feel threatened by Paulo de Carvalho in Sussex that night, but perhaps the rebel majors saw a perverse logic in choosing a song that had bombed to herald the start of an uprising.

There was nothing remotely political about the song. It was a sub-Sinatra effort lamenting the end of a relationship with the singer comparing his lover to a flower he had picked. The implication therefore was that the relationship was wilting and would not last long, unless he was also suggesting that she had a nasty infestation of greenfly. 'E Depois do Adeus' was duly played on the radio station Emissores Associados de Lisboa at 10.50 pm on the evening of 24 April to alert the rebel leaders and soldiers to begin the coup.

As thousands took to the streets in support of the military insurgents, Caetano caved in. It was all over in six hours and was dubbed the Carnation Revolution, partly because scarcely a shot had been fired but also because the people took to the streets to celebrate and inserted carnations from Lisbon flower market into the muzzles of rifles. This was seen more as a symbolic gesture of peace than an indication that there was a serious shortage of vases in the capital.

Every year, the Portuguese celebrate 25 April as Freedom Day. As co-founder of the Sheiks (Portugal's answer to the Beatles), Carvalho is also still remembered fondly although it was his unintentional role in the overthrow of a dictatorship that has assured him of his place in Eurovision history.

YOU CAN'T BRING THAT
GUN IN HERE (1975)

Portugal's 1975 entry '*Madrugada*' ('Dawn') described the joy felt in the country following the successful Carnation Revolution. To underline the point, singer Duarte Mendes, an army lieutenant who had taken part in the revolution, wanted to walk on stage in Stockholm wearing military uniform and carrying a gun. He was strongly advised against doing so and ended up performing in an ordinary jacket and trousers without a holster in sight. He did, however, manage to sneak a symbolic carnation into his buttonhole. The political overtones of the song failed to capture the voters' imagination and it finished sixteenth out of nineteen.

This was the first year of the voting system that endures to this day (give or take a few tweaks) and it seemed to confuse Swedish host Karin Falck, who exclaimed, 'How much is seven in French?' The multilingual Katie Boyle would never have got her knickers in such a twist – assuming that she was wearing any. There was also disquiet outside in the streets of Stockholm, where left-wing demonstrators objected to the show being staged in their city because they thought Eurovision was too commercial. So on the night of the contest, they staged an alternative, protest festival in another part of the city, where anyone could perform, regardless of musical talent, which, ironically, made it much like Eurovision.

Unsurprisingly, the year's winning song, 'Ding Dinge Dong', performed by Teach-In for the Netherlands, was very much in the ABBA vein. Except that its lyrics were pitiful. It began: 'When you're feeling all right, everything is uptight, try to sing a song that goes ding ding-a-dong. There will be no sorrow when you sing tomorrow and you walk along with your ding-dang-dong.' Quite apart from the fact that clinical tests have yet to prove that singing 'ding ding-a-dong' is an effective cure for manic depression, even in the carefree seventies you *were* likely to feel sorrow if you walked along with your ding-dang-dong because you would almost certainly be arrested for indecent exposure.

TURKEY BASHING (1976)

The 1976 Eurovision in the Hague is chiefly remembered for the winning act, the UK's Brotherhood of Man, and the sickeningly twee 'Save Your Kisses For Me'. Its defenders say it is catchy; so was the black death. But behind the cloying jingle and the sight of four grown-ups performing an embarrassing dance routine, that year's contest hid an altogether more sinister, political side, sparked by Turkey's invasion of Cyprus two years previously.

Turkey first appeared at the Eurovision in 1975 and Greece withdrew from the competition. The Greek absence was initially attributed to 'unknown reasons' but it soon emerged that it was in protest at the Turkish invasion of Cyprus. For 1976, Greece decided to voice its protests through the medium of popular song, its entry '*Panagia Mou, Panagia Mou*', written and sung by Mariza Koch, being a savage indictment of Turkish foreign policy in Cyprus. When the Turks heard it, it was their turn to withdraw from the contest. Turkish TV went ahead and televised the final, but in place of the Greek entry it substituted a nationalistic Turkish song, '*Memleketim*' ('My Motherland').

'*Panagia Mou, Panagia Mou*' (which translates as 'My Lady, My Lady') sings of 'a lucid land ... goldened with sun' (Cyprus) where the tents among the trees are no longer for tourists but for refugees. It warns, 'And should you stand up on some ruins – don't cry, oh mother, they won't be remains left there from ancient times. They're homes burnt down by napalm bombs . . . by darksome kinds.'

In a year when the juries were more impressed by a dad singing to his three-year-old, an earnest political song had little chance of success and '*Panagia Mou, Panagia Mou*' finished thirteenth out of the eighteen countries taking part. Even so, Greece had made its point.

TEARS OF A CLOWN (1976)

Clowns can be divisive figures. A lot of people find them only marginally more amusing than root canal surgery while others have an active phobia of clowns. For Eurovision in the 1970s, however, clowns were fun and loveable – nothing remotely spooky or sinister about them. So it came to pass that Swiss trio Peter, Sue and Marc sang 'Djambo, Djambo', a pleasant little song about a retired clown, once 'the best that ever was' but now living on faded memories. It brings a tear to the eye just thinking about it. In the filmed introduction, the three were pictured skipping joyously across a bridge, no doubt to remind us of Djambo in happier times.

In the early years, Eurovision performers just stood there in either gowns or suits but now costumes and props were beginning to feature and Peter, Sue and Marc were supported by a man dressed as a clown at a barrel organ. When it came to the chorus, he picked up a guitar but stopped short of hurling a bucket of water over the conductor. 'Djambo, Djambo' was received with such warmth that it finished fourth overall with the UK jury awarding it the maximum *douze points*. This was one of Peter, Sue and Marc's four appearances at the Eurovision Song Contest and each time they sang in a different language: French (1971), English (1976), German (1979) and Italian (1981). In most of the intervening years, they tried to win the nomination but failed. They were nothing if not keen.

Meanwhile the Les Humphries Singers, representing Germany, fell foul of the contest's 'six items or fewer' rule. There were twelve members in all but only half of them were allowed to perform 'Sing, Sang, Song', the lyrics of which basically consisted of repeating the title over and over again. It would have been preferable if all twelve had appeared and sung only half the song. Finland offered Fredi and Friends' 'Pump-Pump', which encouraged you to 'let your hip go hippety-pump-pump' while you dance. Seeing that Fredi weighed over seventeen stone, he might not have had many friends left if his hip went hippety-pump-pump too often on the dance floor.

At the conclusion of the voting, the scoreboard showed Yugoslavia as being last of the eighteen countries on six points, courtesy of one from Switzerland, two from Germany and three from Greece. Long after everyone had gone home, somebody noticed that the spokesperson of the French jury had forgotten to award four points to anyone. These, it transpired, should have gone to Yugoslavia. So the scoring was retrospectively altered, giving Yugoslavia ten points and thereby relegating Norway to last place – a position with which it had become all too familiar and would be again.

SATIRE COMES TO EUROVISION (1977)

The 1977 contest at the Wembley Conference Centre was postponed for five weeks due to a strike by BBC technicians. Rumour has it that the militants only returned to work when they heard that Greece had a particularly catchy entry for the Eurovision. When else would they get a chance to wear their satin shirts, gold medallions and white flares? Certainly not at the TUC conference. It was also the year that satire arrived at the Eurovision thanks to the Austrian entry 'Boom Boom Boomerang' performed by the five members of Schmetterlinge.

The entire song sent up past winners such as 'Boom Bang-A-Bang' and 'Ding Dinge Dong' with a nonsensical chorus which ran, 'Boom boom boomerang, snadderydang, kangaroo, boogaloo, didgeridoo.' To emphasise the point that the song was not intended to be taken seriously, the four male singers, wearing cream suits and red shirts, periodically turned their backs to the audience, revealing a costume which looked like the front of a tuxedo, complete with a fake face. They held banknotes to represent the vast amounts of money that record companies could expect to make from such drivel. Alas for Schmetterlinge, the worthy sentiments were not backed up by even a passable tune and the subversive Austrians finished seventeenth in a field of eighteen, with just eleven points.

At least that was probably their position, because the voting, announced by newsreader Angela Rippon, descended into chaos. Greece set the ball of confusion rolling by awarding four points to two different countries, Spain and Austria, without anybody spotting the error. (Where was Katie Boyle when you needed her?) Next, Israel omitted to announce to whom it was awarding four points but luckily that oversight was corrected. Voting last, France, who had already won the contest and had therefore probably been hitting the bubbly, got its scores for Portugal and Italy the wrong way round before proceeding to give three points to two countries, Greece and Israel, and one point each to Belgium and Austria. Again, nobody noticed, so at the end of the show half of the eighteen countries had incorrect totals on the scoreboard. These were later adjusted, but by then everyone was long past caring.

AN EPIC *NUL POINTS* (1978)

Most Eurovision acts achieved fame and fortune by winning the contest, but Norway's Jahn Teigen opted for a different approach. He became a national hero, alongside the likes of Amundsen, Munch and Grieg, by finishing last without a single vote to his name – the first artist to achieve the dreaded *nul points* under the current voting system.

In the UK, the ignominy would have seen him consigned to the ranks of occasional guest presenter on *Play School,* while in the USSR he would probably never have been seen again in public, but the Norwegians actually embraced his failure. The fateful song, '*Mil Etter Mil*' ('Mile After Mile'), went on to top the national singles chart for two months and remained in the Top 10 for three more. His follow-up single, the aptly titled 'I Won't Give Up', hung around the Norwegian charts for the rest of the year, also helping sales of his album, *This Year's Loser.* He was even selected to represent his country at the Eurovision on two more occasions. In 1982 he finished a more respectable twelfth with a duet he sung with his wife Anita Skorgan, 'Adieu', and in 1983 he went solo again to come ninth with 'Do Re Mi'. Although that was his last Eurovision appearance, it was not for the want of trying. He has taken part in the Norwegian national Eurovision final, the *Melodi Grand Prix*, on no fewer than fourteen occasions, the most recent in 2005. Some people are just gluttons for punishment.

Re-watching the performance from that night in Paris in 1978, it is hard to decide which was worse: the song or Jahn Teigen. He was already established in Norway first with the rock band Popol Ace and then as a comedy musician with the trio Prima Vera and was seen as something of a character. To underline the point, when he sang 'Voodoo' at the 1976 *Melodi Grand Prix*, he wore a skeleton suit. He left no one in any doubt that, had the song made it through to that year's Eurovision, he would have worn that same suit and the rest of Europe would have chuckled at those wacky Norwegians.

Two years later, he was second to perform. Ireland had been the first act, prompting Clive James to write in the *Sunday Times* that the show 'began with an Irishman called C.T. Wilkinson, who proclaimed "I Was Born to Sing". How wrong can you be?' In Teigen's camp, there was a quiet confidence about '*Mil Etter Mil*', although at least one Norwegian TV executive harboured grave reservations about Teigen's chosen outfit. His suggestion that Teigen should change clothes fell on deaf ears. So it was that the singer took to the stage looking worryingly like a punk Larry Grayson in braces. That these were a prop rather than just an outfit became apparent when he proceeded to twang them during the performance, which he rounded off by doing the splits in mid-air. Excruciating barely covers it.

Pre-contest optimism dropped like a very large stone with voting. As nation after nation delivered its damning verdict on the Norwegian effort, it was suggested to Teigen that he might actually be better off to score no points than just a handful. When the twentieth nation, Sweden, followed the rest of Europe by studiously ignoring its neighbour, that wish was granted. Finland fared little better, acquiring a total of just two points, which were awarded in the second round of voting by . . . Norway. If the Norwegian jury had, like everyone else, failed to see any merit in the Finnish entry, Jahn Teigen's post-Eurovision career would surely have been far less successful. As it was, he was able to call his achievement 'the proudest moment of my life'. For once, he wasn't joking.

SAY IT WITH FLOWERS (1978)

If Jahn Teigen was a popular loser in 1978, the same could not be said of the winner, Israel's Izhar Cohen and Alphabeta with 'A-Ba-Ni-Bi'. The song itself was fairly typical Eurovision nonsense but Jordanian TV refused to show the actual performance, cutting instead to a picture of a bunch of daffodils. When it then became apparent that Israel was going to win, most of the Arabic TV stations showing the live contest ended their broadcast early, claiming technical difficulties. Jordan's JTV subsequently told viewers that Belgium had won. In fact, Belgium had finished thirty-two points behind Israel in second place, so this was definitely a case of wishful thinking.

Bizarrely, the winning song was not even appreciated in its homeland. Singer and broadcaster Rivka Michaeli dismissed it as a children's song that was unrepresentative of the best of Israeli music. She said that it was only because all of the other entries were so 'absolutely awful' that Cohen had won the national heats.

Such criticism did not deter Cohen from trying to repeat his success but, in 1985, performing 'Olé Olé' (again backed by Alphabeta), he could finish only fifth. He attempted to represent Israel again in 1987 and 1996 but faltered in the national final.

HISTORIC HORRORS (1979)

**Whereas Portugal opted for safety at the 1979 contest in Jerusa-
lem with a song about balloons, Germany and Greece both
decided to explore the historical route in the hope of creating an
artistic oasis in what is traditionally a cultural desert.**

Taking several leaves out of Boney M's 'Rasputin', German
six-piece Dschinghis Khan performed a flamboyant disco number
in praise of the thirteenth-century Mongol warlord better known
to us as Genghis Khan. Instead of 'Ra, Ra, Rasputin', they sang
'Geng, Geng, Genghis Khan'. Spot the difference. Far from pour-
ing scorn on his habit of butchering thousands of people as he
and his armies rampaged across Asia, the song portrayed him as
good old Genghis, mighty warrior and sex machine. The lyrics
particularly focused on his way with women: 'And every woman
that he liked, he took into his tent. It's said that there wasn't a
woman in the world who didn't love him. He fathered seven children in one night.' Whaddaguy!

To put their message across, the four men in the band strutted
bare-chested with front man, Louis Potgieter, giving an approxi-
mate impersonation of Genghis, although it is debatable whether
the latter would have instilled such terror into his victims had he,
too, been wearing a pair of gold lamé trousers. Some felt that a

song extolling the virtues of violence and military strength was not a desirable image for Germany in Israel, but the disco movement was still lively enough in Europe for 'Dschinghis Khan' to finish fourth overall with Israel itself awarding it six points.

Greece chose a more cerebral figure as the subject for their entry: fifth-century philosopher Socrates. Philosophy tends not to lend itself to a disco beat in the same way as mass rape and murder, so popular Greek singer Elpida was slightly more restrained with her tribute to 'Socrates superstar'. 'Dressed in a gown, you walked through the town, Socrates, first superstar.' She went on to explain that he was so clever his enemies wanted him dead, and he came across in the song as a thoroughly decent bloke who at least didn't drag women into his tent whenever he felt the urge. 'Sokrati' came eighth.

Austria got in on the act with *'Heute in Jerusalem'* ('Today in Jerusalem'), a demand for peace in the Middle East performed by jazz singer Christina Simon. Despite its noble intentions, it finished last. Israel won for the second successive year, with 'Hallelujah' (performed by Milk and Honey), while the UK, represented by Black Lace singing 'Mary Ann', trailed in seventh. It would be another five years before they unleashed 'Agadoo' onto an unsuspecting world – one of the few songs too lowbrow even for Eurovision.

DETAINED AT CUSTOMS (1979)

Switzerland's Peter, Sue and Marc were at it again with their props in 1979 and this time it nearly backfired on them. They were detained at Israeli customs and had to explain why they needed to bring a pedal bin, watering can, dustbin lids, garden rake, shears, a hose and window blinds into the country for the Eurovision Song Contest. The sad truth is that they were improvised instruments for use in their song, 'Trödler and Co', which was about a second-hand shop. In it they were supported by another musical threesome, Pfuri, Gorps and Kniri, but as everyone knows, the only good things from Switzerland that come in threes are family packs of Toblerone.

(HYDROELECTRIC)
POWER TO THE PEOPLE (1980)

You have to hand it to the Norwegians; fear of failure is clearly not a national trait. Why else would they choose as their entry for the 1980 Eurovision a song about the construction of a hydro-electric power plant? Its inspiration was the controversial build-ing of a power station on the Alta river in northern Norway which led to activists among the Sami people of Lapland conducting a hunger strike in front of the Norwegian parliament building. Worthy though it may be, it is not exactly a subject that has Euro-vision winner stamped all over it. It is doubtful, for example, whether Bucks Fizz would have enjoyed the same success a year later singing about the Liverpool cemetery workers' strike of 1979. It's not only the subject matter of '*Sámiid Ædnan*' ('Sami Earth') that is questionable – the song itself is a curious mishmash of different styles. It mixes folk, brass bands and unenthusiastic yodelling in the hope of somehow finding a tune.

It was performed by Sverre Kjelsberg and Mattis Hætta. It starts with Kjelsberg, who also wrote the number, strumming the guitar alone on stage until after over a minute Hætta appears, prompting gasps from the audience along the lines of, 'Oh, no, there's two of them.' Hætta's contribution is yoik – a form of vocal

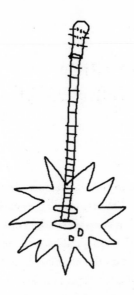

music without words that is apparently popular among the Sami people. In the lyrics, yoik is described as being 'stronger than gunpowder'. It would have been nice to have tested the theory on the night. At one point the orchestra does its best to drown the duo out but sadly doesn't quite succeed. That it finished sixteenth out of nineteen countries says a lot about the ineptitude of Belgium, Morocco and Finland that year.

BITING THE HAND
THAT FEEDS YOU (1980)

If the Norwegian entry for 1980 was ill-judged, the Belgium offering was positively suicidal – a song which, like the Austrians three years earlier, sent up the Eurovision Song Contest. 'Euro-Vision', by Telex, was a cheery little synth-pop number with deliberately banal lyrics designed to expose the whole competition as a meaningless exercise. The audience in the Hague seemed unsure how to react to the song, which was performed in a robotic, Kraftwerk-like manner. The conclusion was greeted by a mixture of stunned silence and scattered polite applause. Band member Michel Moers took a photo of the bewildered faces as the trio trooped off.

An indication of the confusion caused by the song came when Greece awarded it three points. The announcer thought she must have misheard and gave the points to the host country before the error was spotted. But 'Euro-Vision' needed all the help it could get. It eventually finished seventeenth with just fourteen votes – a mere 129 points behind Johnny Logan's winning number, 'What's Another Year?' Telex were dismayed, but not for the reasons most acts might cite. 'We had hoped to finish last,' confessed lead singer Marc Moulin, 'but Portugal decided otherwise and gave us ten points.'

IF YOU WANNA SEE SOME MORE (1981)

Just as people are often asked where they were when Kennedy was shot (although now that *New Tricks* has been cancelled, an alibi is no longer needed), Eurovision fans still ask each other, 'Where were you when Bucks Fizz ripped off their skirts?' Yet it is frankly disturbing to think that one of the contest's most memorable moments nearly never happened – all because Cheryl Baker was worried about displaying her muscular legs to an audience of millions.

Baker had previous at Eurovision as a member of Co-Co in 1978. Great things were expected of that UK entry but 'The Bad Old Days' could finish no higher than eleventh, leaving Baker feeling 'totally disillusioned, that I'd let the country down. I can't honestly say I enjoyed anything about my first Eurovision experience even though it had been a childhood ambition. Dublin in 1981, however, was a completely different kettle of fish.'

What made the fish in her kettle so different with Bucks Fizz was a belting song, 'Making Your Mind Up', and *that* skirt routine. Although almost every member of the group has, at one time or another, laid claim to coming up with the idea, the most credible inventor is choreographer Chrissy Wickham. It came about because neither Baker nor the other girl singer, Jay Aston, could agree on what length of skirt they should wear. 'I had muscular runner's legs,' said Baker, 'and I wanted a long skirt but Jay was very tiny so she wanted short. We were going to-and-fro for ages and then someone said, "Let's have both," and Chrissy said she could make that work. The skirts had a buckle on them that the boys [Bobby G and Mike Nolan] grabbed to make the longer skirt come away and reveal the shorter one underneath. It was the iconic moment that won us the competition; I really believe that.'

Wickham says, 'There's a line that goes, "If you wanna see some more", and it just seemed like the perfect point to me. It's so obvious in a choreographer's mind. It was also just before the jive sequence, which they didn't need big skirts for, so it was a good point to remove the longer ones. Unfortunately, the magic has gone out of it now because everyone keeps trying to claim credit for it.'

The voting proved incredibly close and, with two rounds to go, it was a three-way tie between the UK, Germany and Switzerland, who had yet to vote. When the Swiss jury awarded eight points to the UK but none to Germany in the penultimate round, victory was within touching distance. Bucks Fizz won by four points. Velcro's finest moment had tilted the balance.

The group enjoyed tremendous success over the next few years but a devastating coach crash, which almost killed Nolan, was followed by endless line-up changes and internal legal disputes. Founder members went off in all directions. It was even said that if you stood at a certain point in Derbyshire you could see five counties and three different incarnations of Bucks Fizz.

VOTES, WHAT VOTES? (1981)

The most entertaining part of a Eurovision evening – particularly in the early years – was invariably the voting. Audiences would sit at home watching a little black-and-white TV set, marvelling at how modern technology enabled distant European cities to be instantly contacted. Or not contacted. For, all too often, the studio host's request for a nation's votes would be met with either total silence or an incomprehensible crackling that made it sound as if the spokesperson was frolicking gaily in a field of bubble wrap or was in the process of electrocuting themselves. Since the show's presenter could never be certain that there was going to be someone on the other end of the line, the jury spokesperson was often addressed in the way that a frustrated mother would speak to an errant child. 'Can you hear me, Helsinki?' 'Are you there, Monaco?' 'Don't do that, Copenhagen, or you won't get any tea.'

Alas, these days the voting has lost some of its charm. This is partly due to fewer communication breakdowns and also because so many countries now take part that voting seems to drag on forever despite the organisers' attempts to condense it. Another irritating development is the way the juries feel obliged to preface their results with fulsome praise for the host nation's show, delivered with all the sincerity of a used-car salesman.

In 1981 – back when voting was still haphazard – trouble began with the very first jury, Austria. It opened its results by awarding five points to Germany. This prompted the European Broadcasting Union scrutineer, Frank Naef, to issue Austria with a firm reprimand: 'You should start with the ascending order. I can't understand why you start with five.' For Vienna, this reprimand was like being sent to its room.

When Luxembourg voted, its ten points for Ireland showed up on the scoreboard as 310, which might have brought the evening to a premature – and, for some, a welcome – end. Turkey's score kept reverting to zero – not actually far from the truth as it only managed a final total of nine – but the biggest laugh of the night was reserved for Yugoslavia. After repeated failed attempts to contact Belgrade, Irish host Doireann Ní Bhriain finally succeeded in getting through to jury spokesperson Helga Vlahović, who, when asked for her country's votes, answered curtly, 'I don't have it.' There then followed an awkward interlude between Dublin and Belgrade that resembled a conversation between two deaf aunts before Vlahović suddenly delivered her votes. She had them all along. What a tease!

NO TURKISH DELIGHT (1981)

Cyprus made its Eurovision debut in 1981, an event that did not exactly go down well with Turkey. Not only did each country pointedly fail to award the other a single point, but when the Cypriot song – 'Monika', by five-piece band Island – was performed, Turkish TV instantly cut to a commercial break. To make things worse, Cyprus finished sixth and Turkey joint eighteenth. The feud would rumble on for years.

NUCLEAR PROTEST (1982)

Not to be outdone by their Scandinavian neighbours' hydro-electric power plant song, Finland scored *nul points* in 1982 with '*Nuku Pommiin*' ('Ban the Bomb'), a protest about the building of a nuclear weapons base. The song suggests that the best way to survive a nuclear attack is to stay in bed and sleep through it, although there is no indication that this assertion is based on any firm scientific evidence. The opening lines are among the more distinctive Eurovision offerings: 'If someone soon throws some nuclear poo here on our Europe, what will you say when we got all the filth on our faces?' No one was ever going to mistake it for 'Puppet on a String'.

Selected as Finland's entry at the expense of the more conventional 'My Apple Tree', '*Nuku Pommiin*' was written by Englishman Jim Pembroke and sung by Kojo (Finnish pop star Timo Kojo) in a distinctive red leather suit, clearly hoping that his outfit would help the audience forget about the song. For not only did the subject matter have limited to zero appeal for Eurovision viewers, it was also sung in Europe's most impenetrable language. If the audience in genteel Harrogate were dumbstruck, heaven knows what they made of it in Nicosia or Istanbul. Backed by a four-piece band dressed like the Helsinki branch of the Blues Brothers, Kojo delivered the incongruously upbeat tune while hitting himself over the head every time he reached the chorus. Sadly, it was never hard enough to knock him unconscious and prevent him finishing the song.

He subsequently admitted to Tim Moore, author of the splendid book *Nul Points*, that it was an 'all-or-nothing song. We hear the others in rehearsal, and we are so different, we know we either win or lose.' There was never any doubt that the answer would be lose, with Kojo failing to register as much as a flicker of interest among the voting panels of the other seventeen countries.

NOT GOOD ENOUGH (1982)

When it comes to quality standards in Eurovision, it is tempting to think that the bar is set so low it almost touches the ground, but in 1982 Greece evidently had loftier ideals. It was supposed to go to Harrogate with the song '*Sarantapente Kopelies*' performed by Themis Adamantidis. Just two weeks before the contest, the country's minister of culture, Melina Mercouri – herself a successful singer – suddenly announced Greece's withdrawal, stating that the song did not meet her strict measurement of quality. This may have been a convenient excuse for there was a suggestion that the song, being a revival of a Greek folk number, violated Eurovision rules because it was not original. Also, as Mimis Plessas, who conducted the orchestra for the 1983 Greek entry, testified, Mercouri was none too keen on the Eurovision Song Contest anyway. The clue to her stance might just be in her job title.

A NIGHT AT THE OPERA (1983)

The Spanish entry for the 1983 contest in Munich was '*Quién Maneja Mi Barca?*' ('Who Sails My Boat?'), performed by flamenco singer Remedios Amaya in a vortex-patterned, blue-and-white striped outfit guaranteed to give viewers a headache. It has been described as a tent made out of Greek flags.

Like Sandie Shaw before her, Amaya performed the song in bare feet. It is not certain whether the shoeless option was a result of not being able to find any footwear in the whole of Spain that complemented her costume (and this is entirely plausible) or whether someone thought that, because it had worked once sixteen years earlier, the gimmick must be a sure-fire vote-winner. But whereas Shaw left clutching the trophy, Amaya left clutching nothing more than sore feet, having failed to earn a single point from the other European juries. Yet that year's competition is best remembered for her fellow *nul point*-er, Turkey's Çetin Alp, whose song 'Opera' has often been hailed as the worst in Eurovision history.

Composed by Buğra Uğur with words by Aysel Gürel, 'Opera' was certainly different. The native language rule was back in force at the time in Eurovision (and would be until 1998), but short quotations from another language were permissible provided they were 'no longer than one phrase'. So to get around the fact that Turkish was not exactly a language that travelled well, the writers honed in on an easily understood theme, opera, and bludgeoned listeners over the ears with it.

A booming ballad performed by a bespectacled baritone, 'Opera' repeated the title twenty-seven times interspersed with sudden inexplicable outbreaks of 'Lay, lay, lay'. The lyrics also name checked Wagner, Puccini, Mozart and Rossini, along with celebrated opera titles that were short enough to fit into what passed as a tune. The hapless Alp was supported in his endeavours by the Short Waves – five backing vocalists ludicrously dressed as operatic characters. A short wave was just about the sum total of their reception. Nobody who witnessed the spectacle could have been overly surprised when 'Opera' failed to trouble the scoreboard.

For Alp, it was downhill all the way after that. Burdened by the shame he felt he had brought upon his country – although in truth there was not much more he could have done with the song – he all but disappeared from public view. He died – some might say for a second time – three days after the 2004 Eurovision Song Contest.

LOST IN TRANSLATION (1983)

The host in Munich, leggy dancer Marlene Charell, was asked to demonstrate her linguistic skills by announcing each vote in three languages (German, English and French) instead of the usual two. This meant that the voting went on for over an hour, extending the length of the show to more than three hours for the first time ever. The following programme *Match of the Day* was in serious danger of becoming *Match of Yesterday*.

A series of embarrassing blunders followed as sheer fatigue took hold. Those who take delight in counting such things have found a total of twenty-seven slip-ups by Charell on the night, including thirteen mistakes during the voting. One of her finest moments was falteringly introducing Norwegian conductor Sigurd Jansen as 'Johannes Skorgan', a Scandinavian-sounding name made up on the spot after totally forgetting the conductor's identity. Thereafter, the evening degenerated into one of abject confusion that demonstrated little of the famed German efficiency. She mixed up Israel and Italy, nearly gave twelve points instead of two to France and got her multilingual tongue so tied that points for Switzerland ('*Schweiz*') were almost awarded to Sweden ('*Schweden*'). Charell was also the interval act that year. She could have done with the rest.

WOGAN'S HEROES (1984)

Terry Wogan was synonymous with the Eurovision Song Contest in the UK for nearly forty years. He first provided the BBC's radio commentary for the event in 1971 before switching to television for a sardonic stint lasting from 1980 until 2008, by which time, even though he had not quite run out of countries and performers to mock, he decided to call it a day. So when Wogan said that one particular song is the worst at Eurovision – and let us not forget how fierce the competition is in that particular category – the world had to sit up and take notice. Take a bow Sweden's 1984 entry, 'Diggi-Loo Diggi-Ley'.

It was performed by three clean-cut Mormon brothers, Per, Richard and Louis Herrey, calling themselves Herreys. Comparisons with the Osmonds were welcomed. Tommy Körberg, who represented Sweden in the 1969 and 1988 contests, dubbed Herreys 'the dancing deodorants', a derogatory nickname that stuck with them in their home country. The song's title gave every indication of the nonsense to come. The lyrics related a dream of the lead singer in which he finds a pair of golden shoes in the street. When he puts them on, he immediately feels like dancing and believes he can achieve whatever he wants in life. The chorus runs, 'Diggi-loo diggi-ley, let this miracle stay, I could be whatever

I would choose, please don't wake me up, I'm dreamin' of me in golden shoes.' It was cheesier than a wheel of cheddar but the boys performed it with great gusto from the tops of their coiffed hair right down to the toes of their golden boots. With all these Eurovision credentials in place, it was not altogether surprising that with the help of maximums from Cyprus, Ireland, Denmark, Austria and Germany, 'Diggi-Loo Diggi-Ley' romped to victory.

It seems sacrilegious to disagree with Sir Terence but I feel there have been many worse songs than 'Diggi-Loo Diggi-Ley' at Eurovision – indeed many worse winners. Perhaps it was the golden boots that put him off. It was not really a look that would have suited him.

NOT THE BELLE OF THE BALL (1984)

For all its faults, the Eurovision Song Contest is generally quite a civilised affair – more akin to performing at an end-of-the-pier show than in a hostile bear pit. A poor song will generally be greeted by nothing worse than muted applause and mild indifference. A rare exception came in 1984 when UK girl group Belle and the Devotions suffered the fate of being booed off by a section of the audience in Luxembourg. Their song, 'Love Games', owed so much to Tamla Motown that it turned them into a white Supremes tribute act while their big hair, short skirts and gaudy lime-green-and-black outfits suggested that Lily Savage's personal stylist may also have been an influence. In the build-up to the event, there were unfounded rumours of plagiarism and that two of the girls were not actually singing and these false stories may have poisoned some people against 'Love Games'. However, it has also been claimed that the real reason why Belle and the Devotions were jeered had nothing to do with either their singing (or lack of it) or the song – it was a reaction to recent disgraceful behaviour of English football hooligans in Luxembourg. The Luxembourg jury reflected these sentiments by awarding the song just one point and, with the rest of Europe only marginally less scathing, it limped home seventh.

WARDROBE MALFUNCTION (1985)

The 1985 contest in Gothenburg had more UK male viewers than usual when it was noticed that the Swedish entry, to be performed by Kikki Danielsson, was titled '*Bra Vibrationer*'. So imagine my, sorry, *their* disappointment when it translated as 'Good Vibrations' and was nothing more salacious than a love song about a woman's new relationship. Still, the Swedes did not totally disappoint with a stunt that briefly (if you'll pardon the word) revealed presenter Lill Lindfors in her underwear.

Lindfors, who had sung for Sweden back in 1966, wore a skirt for the first half of the show but when she walked back on stage after the interval to prepare for the voting, she contrived to catch the garment on a nail, pulling the skirt away and leaving her in just her knickers and the top half of her dress. She pretended to be shocked for a few seconds while gasps were heard across Europe and then coolly unfastened the flaps of her dress across her shoulders to create a full-length white gown. As the penny dropped, she told the audience, 'I just wanted to wake you up a little.' This is always a sensible precaution after any Eurovision interval act.

She later confirmed that the trick had been pre-planned but that she had not performed it at rehearsals the night before, presumably for fear of falling foul of the Eurovision censors. As it was, the stunt is said to have left the wife of EBU scrutineer Frank Naef less amused than Queen Victoria watching a music-hall routine taking the piss out of the late Prince Albert.

Breaking the habit of a lifetime, the winner that year was Norway with '*La Det Swinge*' ('Let It Swing') sung by female duo Bobbysocks!, who were congratulated on their victory by Lindfors. 'I am honestly very happy that this happened because Norway has been last on so many times that you really deserve it!" she smiled. She thus managed to congratulate Norway while at the same time neatly reminding it of its place in the Scandinavian pecking order.

EMPTY THREATS (1987)

Five years after Melina Mercouri put her foot down over the Greek entry, another country's minister of culture tried to influence a Eurovision selection. This time it was Israel's minister, Yitzhak Navon, who felt that his country's entry, *'Shir Habatlanim'* ('The Bums' Song') by the Lazy Bums (comedy duo Datner and Kushnir), was an unworthy representation of Israeli music. The song described a lazy bum's day with a chorus that went: 'Hupa hule hule hule hupa hupa hule hule hupa hule hule hupa pa hupa hule hule hupa hupa hule hule hupa hule hule hupa pa ...' Anyway you get the drift. Ultimately the minister's views were ignored, and the song went forward to the final in Brussels where it finished a respectable eighth, albeit light years behind Johnny Logan's winning 'Hold Me Now'. Navon had threatened to resign over the issue but, being a seasoned politician, never did.

In the same year, a minor diplomatic row broke out after BBC radio presenter Ray Moore light-heartedly described the Turkish representatives, Seyyal Taner's backing group Locomotif, as 'an ugly crowd'. He was being rather uncharitable although there was an excessive amount of hair on display. In any case their appearance was the least of their worries because their song, *'Şarkım*

Sevgi Üstüne' ('My Song is About Love'), was so unloved that voters put it last with *nul points*. It was performed throughout at a frenetic pace like a video of the Keystone Cops singing New Pickettywitch. Taner later blamed the conductor for destroying the song with his 'crazy, crazy speed'.

NOW I REMEMBER (1988)

Cyprus was forced to pull out of the 1988 contest in Dublin at the last minute after it was discovered that its entry, '*Thimame*' ('I Remember'), was not original. It is one of the ironies of Eurovision that, in an event where so many of the songs are clearly derivative, a rule states that they must be original. It appears that after the draw had been made (Cyprus was scheduled for the un-favoured second position), the writers of 'I Remember', John Vick-ers and Aristos Moskovakis, suddenly remembered having written the song in 1984 and entering it for that year's Cypriot national contest – in which it came third. As a result, the song, which should have been performed by Yiannis Demetriou, was with-drawn from the contest, leaving Greece fretting over to whom it was going to award *douze points*.

CHILD'S PLAY (1989)

After thirteen-year-old Sandra Kim had won the 1986 Euro-vision for Belgium, other nations decided to maximise the cute kid factor and the 1989 final included performances from twelve-year-old Gili Natanael for Israel and eleven-year-old Nathalie Pâque for France. Worried that the next logical step would be singing toddlers, performers pushing a pram on stage or a musical embryo, Eurovision introduced a new rule which stipulated that all acts must be at least sixteen in the year they compete.

Curiously, that year's Austrian and German entries were written by the same people, Dieter Bohlen and lyricist Joachim Horn-Bernges. Both songs were big ballads and went on to finish fifth and fourteenth respectively. The contest was won by Yugoslavia's Riva with 'Rock Me', much to the frustration of Ray Caruana, lead singer of the UK's Live Report (no, me neither) who finished second with 'Why Do I Always Get It Wrong?'. Afterwards, Caruana was reportedly outspoken about losing to what he considered an inferior song. 'Why Do I Always Get It Wrong?' went on to peak at No. 73 in the UK singles chart. Ray Caruana now designs and repairs high-quality handbags in Billericay. It helps to have a thick hide when you're singing at the Eurovision.

SOMETHING AMISS (1989)

With the 1989 contest taking place in Switzerland, it was natural that the interval act should be devoted to recreating the legend of William Tell. It was either that or dancing cuckoo clocks. However, as the producers of *The Golden Shot* would testify, crossbows and live television make for a dangerous cocktail.

The bowman in question was Guy Tell (can't think what inspired his stage name), and after demonstrating his prowess in a series of stunts with the help of his sister in the role of the lovely Debbie McGee, he came to the big climax. His task was to shoot a crossbow bolt into a balloon, triggering a chain reaction of fifteen more automated crossbows – a bit like the game Mouse Trap but more dangerous – with the last one meant to pierce an apple on top of Tell's head. It was a highly complex routine that took five minutes to rig up and explain on the night.

Wogan had to fill in furiously and, after giving us Guy Tell's life story, he mused, 'If it misses, it will be very embarrassing for the Eurovision Song Contest committee.'

Never was a truer word spoken in jest, for when the bolt was finally fired, it quite clearly missed the apple on Tell's head. Cue an instant action replay, where, lo and behold, before you could say Bernie the Bolt, the bolt split its target with precision. The editors had craftily substituted the live shot with more successful footage from rehearsals. The committee had taken steps to ensure that they would not be embarrassed by the bolt missing the apple one inch to the left. They were probably just grateful that it hadn't missed the apple by one inch below, when it would have hit Tell straight through the forehead. Now that would have been an interval act to remember.

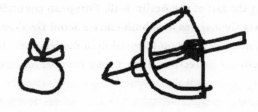

MISSED THEIR CUE (1990)

Following the fall of the Berlin Wall, European countries were falling over themselves to submit entries about freedom, peace and love, making the 1990 Eurovision in Zagreb more an exercise in political correctness than a song contest. Austria's song was titled 'No More Walls', Germany informed us that we were 'Free to Live', Switzerland assured us that 'Music Rings Around the World' and, for the UK, fifteen-year-old Emma (who, born Emma Booth, just scraped through the age rule by having a sixteenth birthday three months later) wanted to 'Give a Little Love Back to the World'. Perhaps worried that the messages were too subtle for Eurovision juries, Norway simply called its song 'Brandenburg Gate'. It was a night when even a song about a hydroelectric power station would have been considered lightweight. After all these earnest political offerings, audiences would actually have been grateful for a 'Bing Tiddle Bong'.

Understandably, light relief was in short supply, but was provided inadvertently by the very first act, Spanish sisters Azúcar Moreno with *'Bandido'* ('Bandit'). A tape technician failed to start the pre-recorded backing track in time, with the result that the two singers, their band, and the orchestra conducted by Eduardo Leiva all missed their cues. The singers started their choreographed dance routine but, as they realised the tape was in the wrong position, they looked at each other blankly, stopped, shrugged, and walked off stage in a huff, leaving viewers to wonder whether they had just witnessed the shortest Eurovision song ever. The band remained on stage, with the guitarist playfully strumming along to the wayward backing track and two minutes later the girls came back out and started all over again. It was a good thing only 200 million people were watching.

CHAOS IN ROME (1991)

The 1991 contest in Rome was co-presented by Italy's only two previous winners, Gigliola Cinquetti from 1964 and the surprise 1990 victor, Toto Cutugno. Miss Cinquetti adapted to the role admirably but was not helped by her sidekick, whose grasp of any language other than Italian was tenuous to say the least. He made Manuel from *Fawlty Towers* sound multilingual. This led to numerous mispronunciations of song titles and artists' and conductors' names until Terry Wogan was eventually heard to sigh, 'It was a sorry day for all of us when this man won last year.'

When it came to the voting, Cutugno spread chaos like a farmer spreading manure. Gesticulating, gurning and gabbling incessantly, he turned the once serene hall into somewhere reminiscent of an Italian airport during a baggage handlers' strike. He mixed up Luxembourg and Portugal, then Switzerland and Greece, and was spectacularly unable to understand any number that was thrown at him from one to twelve.

'It's wonderful to have a compère in charge who's so calm,' added Wogan, tongue so firmly in cheek he was in danger of causing himself facial injury. The state of confusion was not helped when Ankara seemed reluctant to take the call and deliver the Turkish vote. Given the state of the Italian economy, maybe Rome had reversed the charges. When the Turkish spokesperson did finally surface, it sounded as if she was speaking from the bottom of the Black Sea. In despair, Cutugno kept appealing to scrutineer Frank Naef, who ended up acting as an interpreter and announcing the votes in English, followed by Cinquetti in French and, if he felt like it, by Cutugno in Italian. No viewer would have blamed the long-suffering Miss Cinquetti had she suddenly taken an axe to her co-host.

Given Cutugno's ineptitude, Naef and his fellow organizers must have been praying for a straightforward outcome to the voting but, as fate would have it, twenty-two exhausting rounds concluded with Sweden and France finishing in joint first place on 146 points. 'Mr Naef, Mr Naef,' blurted Cutugno, sounding uncannily like Catarella, the bumbling desk sergeant in *Inspector Montalbano*. Patiently, Naef explained that Sweden was the winner. Both countries had received four first-place votes, but Sweden had five second-place votes compared to France's two. This rule had been implemented to avoid a repetition of the 1969 fiasco with its four-way tie. We must just be thankful that Toto Cutugno wasn't involved then and that he has not been required to go compère since.

THE SINGING MULLET (1991)

Toto Cutugno's mastery of geography evidently rubbed off on Yugoslavia, who chose a woman calling herself Baby Doll to sing a number titled 'Brazil' at a European contest. Even a cartwheeling member of her backing troupe couldn't save the song from its Latin-beat suicide and, with Baby Doll looking like someone you might hire for a stag night in Benidorm, it scored a meagre one point on the night. In many years, she would have finished bottom of the pile, but she was spared that ignominy by the presence in the line-up of Austria's Thomas Forstner.

He had made his Eurovision debut in 1989 when, bravely dressed in a lilac bolero jacket with satin lapels and baggy trousers that would not have looked out of place in Bertram Mills' Circus, he finished a creditable fifth. Two years later he received the call again, this time dressed as the purple one from a box of Quality Street. His outfit was topped by a marvellous mullet, the hairstyle – if style is not too strong a word – that was once as essential in Germany's Bundesliga as a pair of football boots. Alas, the golden mane that swept majestically over his twenty-one-year-old neck and down his back could not disguise the fact that his song, '*Venedig im Regen*' ('Venice in the Rain'), was essentially weak and about as enjoyable as a wet weekend in, well, Venice.

Described by Wogan as a 'game little chap', Forstner bounced on stage in Rome fresh-faced, bright-eyed and bushy-tailed, although that might have been the tip of his mullet. His arrival was greeted with cheers; his exit three minutes later was even more eagerly anticipated.

If Austria was disappointed at scoring a big fat zero, Greek singer Sophia Vossou had every right to feel that the orchestra was to blame for her song '*I Anixi*' ('Spring') finishing only thirteenth. The ageing saxophonist was by far the worst culprit, hitting only around half of the correct notes so that his solo sounded like a cat being strangled.

The UK fared little better, with future *EastEnders* actress Samantha Janus singing about starving children while wearing a pink minidress as if she was at the office Christmas party. Penned by Paul Curtis, the man responsible for Emma's sob-fest the year before, 'A Message to Your Heart' was another sentimental offering, this time focusing on the issue of world poverty, complete with the immortal lines: 'Half the world is hungry just through being born and every day is a compromise for a grain of corn.' Corn just about summed it up. The juries of Europe agreed and placed it tenth.

HAVING A BALL (1992)

To select the UK representative for the 1992 Eurovision in Malmö, the BBC dropped the multi-artist format which it had used on *A Song for Europe* **since 1976 in favour of employing one artist to perform all eight nominated songs.** Following an internal selection process which ruled out Michael Fish, Ronnie Corbett and Rod Hull and Emu, the BBC selected Michael Ball, although quite what he had done to deserve it is unclear. Maybe he had been found guilty of taking the last bourbon biscuit at a light-entertainment department function. He went on to finish second in Sweden with 'One Step Out of Time' but afterwards hinted that he may not have totally enjoyed the Eurovision experience: 'I would rather stick pins in my eyes than do that again.'

Finland finished last with Pave Maijanen's 'Yamma, Yamma', a curious, nostalgic song in praise of valve radio and in which 49 per cent of the words were 'yamma'. Still, at least he made it to Malmö, which was more than could be said for Géraldine Oliver, chosen to represent Switzerland with the sunny song *'Soleil, Soleil'* ('Sun, Sun'). The song had originally been performed in French but when it failed to make the final organised by the French-speaking Swiss broadcaster TSR, it was translated into German and entered into the contest of the German-speaking Swiss broadcaster SF. It won the German heat and went on to win the Swiss national final, meaning that it was selected as the Swiss Eurovision entry. At that point, the French-speaking Swiss, who had already rejected the song, protested vehemently and so the second-placed song, 'Mister Music Man', was sent to Sweden in its place. Sung by Daisy Auvray in French despite its English title, it finished fifteenth out of the twenty-three countries.

Another to find the trip to Sweden traumatic was seasoned Eurovision campaigner Dieter Bohlen, who had composed the Austrian song, *'Zusammen Geh'n'* ('Go Together'), to be sung by Tony Wegas. Bohlen lost his rag after his girlfriend had trouble getting her pet dog into Sweden, and it was reported that his working relationship with Wegas came under strain while he tried to sort out the case of the problem pooch. The song finished only tenth but Bohlen reworked it a decade later as the theme for *Deutschland sucht den Superstar*, the German version of *Pop Idol*, and it became a million-seller. As a judge on that show, Bohlen is famous for barbed comments such as 'You sing like a garden gnome on ecstasy' or 'Your voice sounds like Kermit getting his ass kicked.' He makes Simon Cowell sound like Aled Jones but he probably drew the line at sticking pins in contestants' eyes.

BAD DRESS ALERT (1993)

The 1993 Eurovision was staged in a hall normally used for horse auctions in the tiny Irish town of Millstreet. BBC newsreader Nicholas Witchell disparagingly described the venue as 'a cowshed in Ireland', for which he subsequently apologised, if only because he had picked on the wrong ungulate.

Croatia, Slovenia and Bosnia-Herzegovina all made their debuts, the Bosnian team, including singer Fazla, making it to their plane under a hail of gunfire as they temporarily escaped from their war-torn nation to take part. Even so, they had to leave their conductor behind and Ireland's Noel Kelehan agreed to deputise. Unsurprisingly, the Bosnian song, '*Sva Bol Svijeta*' ('The Whole World's Pain'), spoke of 'the whole world's pain in Bosnia tonight'. Unfortunately, the European juries did not share Fazla's pain and voted him down to sixteenth out of twenty-five.

Chirpy Scouse warbler Sonia was the pre-contest favourite and, never lacking in confidence, reportedly bet five hundred pounds on herself to win. In the event, her 'Better the Devil You Know' faded over the final few furlongs and was beaten into second place by the host country's Niamh Kavanagh with 'In Your Eyes'. The celebrations went on all night – not least in the UK, where the result meant we were spared another overdose of Sonia.

Women very much ruled the roost that year with five of the top six places filled by female solo artists. Supporting them all – in as much as she finished last – was Belgium's Barbara (Dex). Her song, *'Iemand Als Jij'* ('Someone Like You') was dull enough, but it is for her frumpy, flesh-coloured dress – made by her own fair hands – that she is most fondly remembered. The only good thing you could say about it is that at least she didn't blame anyone else for the design. In her honour, Dutch website House of Eurovision has, since 1997, presented the annual Barbara Dex award to the worst-dressed performer (male or female) as voted for by the contest's fans. To many Eurovision followers, the award is as keenly contested as its singing sibling.

FRENCH SWEARING (1994)

As a general rule, love, peace and understanding are safe topics for Eurovision songs. Oh, and nature always goes down well, too, especially birds singing and the weather. If you ever find yourself in the position of penning a potential Eurovision number, it's best not to include any shouty swearing. The Sex Pistols would always have been hard pushed to get more than one point out of the Albanian jury. Nevertheless, France's Nina Morato got away with it in 1994.

Her song, '*Je Suis un Vrai Garçon*' ('I'm a Real Boy'), contained the lyric '*Je sais je suis son amour, mais putain, y'a des jours où c'est lourd*', which translates as 'I know I'm his love, but fuck it, there are days which are hard.' Concerns were raised that this contravened Eurovision rules on verbal obscenities but the French sneaked it through, probably because non-French speakers would have thought '*putain*' was a reference to an up-and-coming Russian politician. While school-grade French allows us to translate the title, '*putain*' is rarely a word that crops up in French vocabulary books, although '*Où est la plume de ma putain de tante?*' might have made Friday afternoon lessons more enjoyable. The juries, already confused by a twenty-seven-year-old woman singing that she was a boy, were also none the wiser and elevated the controversial song to seventh.

The songs were almost of secondary importance in Dublin that year for the show was stolen by the seven-minute interval act, *Riverdance*, which became so influential that nobody in Ireland has walked normally since. Hailing a taxi is now impossible.

IRELAND TAKES A DIVE? (1995)

Ireland had long had a problem with the Eurovision Song Contest – in that it couldn't stop winning the thing. After triumphing with Dana in 1970 and Johnny Logan victories in 1980 and 1987, making him the only person to win it twice – indeed the only person to want to win it twice – Ireland recorded a hat-trick of victories from 1992 to 1994. Hosting the contest the following year (as the winning country is obliged to do) is an expensive outlay, and in 1995 it was suggested that Ireland deliberately chose a lousy song, 'Dreamin' ' by Eddie Friel, to avoid having to stage the contest yet again.

Stories circulated that Ireland had first tried this tactic in 1994 with Paul Harrington and Charlie McGettigan. Aged thirty-three and forty-three respectively, they were old in Eurovision terms and no male duo had ever won before. Their song, 'Rock 'n' Roll Kids', harked back to 1962 and was a simple, mellow tune performed in a statuesque manner by two sombrely dressed performers (one sitting at the piano, the other sitting in a chair strumming a guitar) without any orchestral accompaniment. There was no dancing, no bing-bang-bongs and not a pair of purple latex pants in sight. Amid the forced jollity of the other acts this was like a trip to a funeral parlour. It was a sure-fire

Eurovision flop yet it defied all logic and stormed to victory, becoming the first song to score over two hundred points.

So for 1995, Ireland really needed to pull out all the stops to come up with a losing song. 'Dreamin' ' was pleasant but bland and there were dark mutterings that it was uncomfortably similar to an old Julie Felix song, but the fear remained that it might somehow strike a chord with viewers. Then fate intervened when it was given the number-two performance slot, from which no song has ever won. RTE executives must have breathed a collective sigh of relief, and their worst nightmares were avoided when 'Dreamin' ' finished fourteenth.

The rumours that Ireland had sabotaged its own entry inspired a 1996 episode of *Father Ted*, in which Ted and Dougal compose 'My Lovely Horse', which, as a saccharine-sweet, tuneless, repetitive dirge, fitted the Eurovision brief perfectly. Amazingly, it received *nul points*.

Norway triumphed in 1995 by virtually doing away with lyrics. There were only twenty-four words in Secret Garden's haunting 'Nocturne', making it close to an instrumental. The Norwegian language had been one of its major downfalls in the past – along with unsuitable braces and Lapp reindeer-herding calls.

Luxembourg declined to enter because, as that year's European city of culture, it deemed the contest too tacky. Italy also opted out, claiming that it couldn't fit the event into its TV schedule. The story goes that the national broadcaster came to that conclusion shortly after learning that Toto Cutugno was available that night.

A PROCESS OF ELIMINATION (1996)

With nations such as Estonia, Hungary, Lithuania, Poland, Russia, Romania and Slovakia making their debuts in the mid-1990s, the organisers decided to restrict the number of finalists to twenty-three in a bid to stop the broadcast running way over three hours. You can have too much of a good thing – and the same applies to Eurovision. They added a pre-qualifying round in which all twenty-nine entries (only Norway, as the previous year's winner, was exempt) were played to national juries in a non-televised broadcast and the best twenty-two joined Norway in the final in Oslo.

Germany, Denmark, Macedonia, Israel, Hungary and Russia were eliminated, much to their annoyance. Countries who had gone through a lengthy process of national selection suddenly had their efforts dismissed before they had even been shown to an international audience. It was the Eurovision equivalent of being jilted at the altar. Germany felt particularly aggrieved as it had long been a leading financial contributor to the contest.

Another innovation that year – and one which was mercifully short-lived – was the gimmick of having each song in the final introduced by a leading dignitary from that country wishing them good luck. The scheme might have proved worthwhile had all the heads of state or prime ministers been persuaded to take part but there were too many faceless politicians and lowly bureaucrats. For example, it is doubtful whether a good luck message from Virginia Bottomley, the then secretary of state for national heritage, carried any more weight with the UK's performer, Gina G, than one delivered by a spotty youth working behind the counter at her local Burger King. One leader who did make the effort to deliver a good luck message was Ireland's Taoiseach John Bruton and his reward was another runaway Irish win, courtesy of Eimear Quinn's 'The Voice'. This meant that Ireland had to stage the following year's contest – for the fourth time in five years. Oh dear.

A CRAP RAP (1997)

You have to hand it to Kølig Kaj; he was nothing if not brave. At the 1997 Eurovision Song Contest in Dublin, he chose to rap (not particularly well), in Danish, about a guy who had fallen in love with the woman from directory enquiries – and he delivered it wearing spiky, peroxide-blond hair, thick-framed glasses and a baggy pair of leopard-skin-print trousers. He thus achieved the distinction of being only marginally better with the sound off than on. Despite looking like the sort of person you might definitely consider moving away from if he came and sat next to you on a bus, Cool Kaj (the English translation) and his rap, '*Stemmen I Mit Liv*' ('The Voice in my Life'), finished sixteenth, picking up twenty-five votes along the way, although it is worth noting that all but four of these came from friendly Scandinavian neighbours Norway, Sweden and Iceland. Was it the idea of Danish rap that put off the rest of Europe? Maybe, but it was probably the trousers.

It was not a good year all round for the Scandinavian countries. Norway reverted to type by scoring *nul points* with a song about San Francisco, Icelandic gay icon Paul Oscar finished twentieth with a performance that was way too sexual for Eurovision, and Sweden unleashed a tepid boy band, Blond, which made you wonder why it didn't simply bring Herreys out of frozen storage.

Blond wisely kept their coats on throughout their performance so that, if necessary, they could make a quick getaway afterwards.

Croatia fared no better with ENI, its version of the Spice Girls, nor did Austria with Bettina Soriat's 'One Step', a song memorable only for its reference to *Star Trek* in the lines, 'Love is no bounced cheque, bad man. Oh, sex with you passes by as fast as the spaceship *Enterprise*.' It was sex, Jim, but not as we knew it.

CAN YOU LOSE THE ACCENT? (1997)

With the anthemic 'Love Shine a Light', Katrina and the Waves gave the UK its first Eurovision success since Bucks Fizz – and by a winning margin of seventy points. Their career had been going nowhere fast since 'Walking on Sunshine' twelve years earlier, so when they were first approached to submit a song for Eurovision they remembered how well Gina G's 'Ooh Aah . . . Just a Little Bit' had sold the previous year despite only coming eighth and, as lead singer Katrina Leskanich herself put it, said, 'Yes, we have this song called "Love Shine a Light", which we've never put on a record because it's too cheesy, too ABBA, so it would be perfect for you. Good luck finding some little tweety bird to sing it.'

However, with the lure of a record deal dangled carrot-like before them, the band somewhat reluctantly agreed to perform it themselves. 'We felt confident that we had a really good song that would be a hit in its own right, but once you get into the show, you realise that these Eurovision songs are very specific. We even thought that "Love Shine a Light" was a little too good.' The American singer remembers various designers coming in with outfits for her, most of which looked like upholstery on her tall frame. She ended up wearing a jacket – a Donna Karan second – which her sister had sent to her and which had only one shoulder pad. 'So while I was doing the song, I had to remember to lift my left shoulder slightly to even it out with the other.'

More alarming still was when she was asked to tone down her American accent because she was representing the UK. '"You've lived here twenty-five years," they said. "You can do an English accent." And I said, "Look, I'm going to sound like Dick Van-bloody-Dyke if I have to put on an English accent." Why should I?'

Thankfully she stood firm, but the win in Dublin didn't necessarily give the band the desired shot in the arm. 'We didn't know it was going to be our swansong and the killing of us,' said Leskanich after the Waves broke up in 1999. 'We had a good name in Germany, but they told us we'd sold out with Eurovision. We ended up playing the most glamorous rock 'n' roll locations around the world: Bosnia, Estonia, Latvia, Lithuania, Moldova . . . I'm not knocking them, they're nice, but when you're in a band and you think you're quite cool and you end up there doing a cabaret thing with jugglers and trick dogs: reassess.'

DANA'S LET HERSELF GO (1998)

When the name of Israel's Dana International was first announced at the 1998 contest, viewers all over Europe must have gawped at the screen and thought, Blimey, Dana's let herself go! Of course, this turned out not to be the petite Irish colleen of the seventies but Eurovision's first openly transgender turn, who, at least until Conchita Wurst, was also arguably the contest's most famous solo winner.

The selection of the artist born Yaron Cohen to represent Israel was not without controversy, with orthodox Jews protesting vehemently and claiming that she was 'an abomination'. Some even issued death threats, as a result of which she was housed in the one hotel in Birmingham that had a bulletproof room. Her song 'Diva' conveyed hope that the transgender community could find strength through struggle. It was a long way from 'La La La'. Her performance and backstory (Yaron became Sharon in 1993) certainly moved the voters. (For the first time, telephone voting was used en masse, prompting Terry Wogan to remind viewers, 'You'll have nobody to blame but yourself.')

Israel was one point behind Malta's Chiara going into the final round, but Macedonia, making its debut, showed that the general public could be every bit as unpredictable as any jury. Macedonia awarded eight points to Israel, then ten points to the UK's Imaani, with most people assuming that the twelve would go to Malta. Instead there were gasps among the Birmingham audience as Macedonia completely ignored Malta and gave the *douze points* to neighbours Croatia instead. After all these years, we should have known that local loyalties almost always prevail over common sense. When Slovenia, too, had awarded twelve points to Croatia, the gift came with the unsubtle comment, 'I hope they will remember it very well for next year.'

So the crown went to Dana International. 'My victory proves God is on my side,' she said afterwards. 'I want to send my critics a message of forgiveness.' She lived up to the title of her song by delaying her encore performance for several minutes because she insisted on changing into an extravagant feathered dress. Her antics threatened to make Wogan late for his Ovaltine.

MADMAN ON THE LOOSE (1998)

Following Dana International was Germany's Guildo Horn with his band the Orthopaedic Stockings, so named because they supported him. As will be gathered from that witticism, Guildo was quite a card. Pot-bellied and severely balding with long, lank, clown-like hair, he bounced on stage dressed in a cape (subsequently discarded), a turquoise velvet suit and platform shoes. He looked like every girl's worst nightmare in the seventies. He performed his song, '*Guildo Hat Euch Lieb!*' ('Guildo Loves You All!'), with commendable energy, cavorting among the front row of the audience in the manner of one who had only been allowed out on day release. Interaction with the audience is mercifully rare in Eurovision – you would have never caught Brotherhood of Man crowd surfing. The front row in Birmingham included Katie Boyle but, after tentatively approaching her, he seemed to sense that fondling Eurovision royalty would be a step too far so he quickly retreated and then climbed up a gantry to deliver the closing notes from above the stage – literally finishing on a high. Yet his wacky showmanship, which included an inaudible – and therefore pointless – hand-bell ringing break, could not disguise the fact that his song was so lame that, had it been a horse, it would have been put down.

It is hard to imagine quite what persuaded the German public to select the unkempt Horn as its Eurovision representative. Perhaps it was all those taunts about Germans not having a sense of humour – although if he was an example of German mirth it is probably best that they remain serious. While some Germans thought him little more than an embarrassment, others turned him into a cult figure and launched a campaign to propel him to Eurovision glory. Under the new televoting system, nobody was allowed to vote for their own country, which led to busloads of German students crossing into Belgium, the Netherlands and Switzerland so that they could vote for Guildo from there. While much of Europe thought the joke was thinner than Guildo's hair (when it came to the voting, twelve countries ignored the song completely), this latter-day German incursion enabled him to pick up the maximum from Switzerland and the Netherlands and seven from Belgium, elevating him to a flattering finishing position of seventh. Guildo may have loved them all but the feeling was not necessarily reciprocated.

ULRIKA'S GAFFE (1998)

The double act of Terry Wogan and Ulrika Jonsson coped nobly with the arduous role of presenting Eurovision – the broadcasting equivalent of taking a party of dementia sufferers skydiving – until Ulrika called the Netherlands for its votes. The results were announced in vision by Conny Vandenbos, who had represented her country in the 1965 contest. Before reading the scores, Conny wandered off down memory lane to express her sympathy for all the performers. 'You, of course, have taken part,' said Ulrika, seizing on the feed, before adding, 'A long time ago, was it?' Ouch! As soon as the words came out of her mouth, she realised what she had said and desperately tried to backtrack but the mixture of laughter and ironic jeers from the audience told her the damage had already been done. Sadly, there was never a rematch.

PRIDE BEFORE A FALL (1999)

The records show that the 1999 Eurovision Song Contest was won by Sweden's Charlotte Nilsson but the show was stolen – again – by Dana International, albeit this time unintentionally (probably). To present the trophy to Nilsson, Dana Int. wore a long pink and grey dress that was adorned with two huge feather fans dangling from her wrists. Typically understated, in fact. As she picked up the award she theatrically pretended that it was too heavy to lift but then suddenly lost her balance and fell to the floor, dropping the trophy and pulling down one of the winning composers with her. Security on the night in Jerusalem was tight anyway, with orthodox Jews angered by her reappearance at the event. When she slumped to the floor, many present might have feared that she had been shot. However, helped to her feet, she quickly reassured everyone that the only thing hurt was her pride. She appeared to leave the stage looking embarrassed but the publicity from widespread newspaper and television coverage of her fall amply compensated for any emotional bruising. On the scale of celebrity falls, it was good but no Madonna.

With the rule that each country had to sing in one of its national languages abolished once more, fourteen of the twenty-three – including the winner – decided to perform in English, thereby allowing UK viewers to appreciate the full banality of the lyrics for the first time. A notable exception was the Croatian song, 'Marija Magdalena' performed by Doris Dragović, which finished fourth on the night. However, the Norwegian delegation protested that the Croatian entry used synthesised male vocals on the backing track (all vocals had to be performed live on stage) and the EBU later reduced Croatia's score by a third.

Another new rule saw the good old Eurovision orchestra become an optional feature for the host broadcaster (like a musical side salad). In place of the orchestra, every entry was now able to use a backing track, a decision which annoyed traditionalists including dual winner Johnny Logan. He said that the organisers needed a kick up the arse for turning the Eurovision into a karaoke contest. While that may have been a bit of an exaggeration, it would certainly have livened up the opening to the show had one of the three Israeli hosts, glamorous actress Dafna Dekel, kicked off proceedings with a drunken rendition of 'I Will Survive'.

GIVE PEACE A CHANCE (2000)

Following the fuss over Dana International, Israel might have been expected to lie low Eurovision-wise for a couple of years, but instead it came up with four singers who were as controversial as they were bad. PingPong were a two-boy, two-girl ensemble made up of Guy Assif, Ahal Eden, Roy Arad and Yifat Giladi. Judging by their performance, if they had ever paid for singing lessons, they would surely be entitled to a refund.

'*Sameach*' ('Be Happy') repeatedly urged listeners to do exactly that, no easy task when listening to a song with an atmosphere as welcoming as a party where all the beer has run out, you caught your partner having sex with a complete stranger under a pile of coats, and your parents arrived home unexpectedly early. The foursome's dress sense was no better, with one of the boys wearing a pale green safari-style jacket that would have no longer passed as fashionable even on the Isle of Wight, and one of the girls wearing an unflattering dress accompanied by what could be mistaken from a distance as a pair of gumboots. The charity shops of Tel Aviv had obviously done good business. Yet it was not their singing, their choice of clothes or the excruciating song itself that aroused controversy; it was their insistence on waving plastic Syrian flags during their performance as a message of peace. PingPong's sing-song created a ding-dong.

Having beaten eighty-three other entries to win the Israeli nomination (it is hard to imagine that there were eighty-three worse songs in the whole world, let alone just in Israel), PingPong were promptly disowned by their country as soon as they waved the Syrian flags in rehearsal. The chairman of the Israeli Broadcasting Authority said tersely, 'They will compete [in Stockholm], but not on behalf of the Israeli Broadcasting Authority or the Israeli people. They are representing only themselves.' When there were so many other reasons for Israel to disown the band and the song, to snub them for trying to promote peace in the Middle East was truly pathetic. To their credit, PingPong refused to be bullied and waved their flags again when they were the opening act on the night. Sadly, their message fell on deaf ears, mainly because after the first few bars most listeners had inserted their fingers into them. They picked up just seven points – and six of those came from France – to finish twenty-second out of twenty-four.

Denmark's Olsen Brothers won but only after second-placed Russia – beaten by a margin of forty points – protested unsuccessfully that the Danes had used a vocoder to give an electronic sound to Jørgen Olsen's voice during one of the verses. Nice try. Nicki French achieved what was then the UK's worst finishing position of sixteenth with 'Don't Play That Song Again'. Nobody did.

WOGAN OFFENDS A NATION (2001)

In the UK, we always enjoyed Terry Wogan's idiosyncratic humour – indeed, for millions of people his commentary was the sole incentive to watch the Eurovision Song Contest year after year. Well, that and the chance to dress up in an Agnetha wig. But those in Europe unfamiliar with his broadcasting style did not necessarily appreciate his wry remarks, and in 2001 he landed himself in such hot water with the Danes that the BBC felt compelled to issue a grovelling apology.

The targets for his mounting irritation were the evening's two presenters, actor Søren Pilmark and TV-show host Natasja Crone, who, for reasons best known to themselves, elected to make every introduction in the form of rhyming couplets. The idea must have looked very clever on paper but the novelty wore off – very, very quickly. Wogan scarcely hid his contempt and dubbed the pair 'Doctor Death and the tooth fairy', Pilmark being tall and dark-suited with the appearance of a funeral director and she being dressed all in pink. Some Danes failed to see the funny side although Wogan later laughed it off in typical fashion, claiming, 'To this day, I can travel through Copenhagen airport only with a paper bag over my head.'

The row was still simmering in 2008 when Bjørn Erichsen, the Danish director of Eurovision television, moaned, 'The BBC gets a very large audience but it chooses to represent the contest in a certain way. It's something to laugh at. It's something continental. It's a scam. The British like to distance themselves from it. Terry Wogan is a problem because he makes it ridiculous. They take it far more seriously in Sweden. They have a genuine love and respect for it.' More fool them.

BALTIC CARVE-UP (2002)

Voting for your neighbour has long been a proud, scarcely concealed Eurovision tradition. Even if you do nothing else for them over the rest of the year, twelve points at Eurovision can go a long way towards maintaining cross-border harmony. Had the contest been around at the time of World War II, the Belgians might have told Hitler, 'Your armies marched through our country, destroyed our homes and butchered our people, but hey, you gave us *douze points* at Eurovision, so no hard feelings.'

The Scandinavian countries have often been disproportionately generous to one another – not that it has stopped Norway and Finland racking up more than their share of *nul points* – Greece and Cyprus share an annual mutual appreciation society and Spain and Portugal can usually rely on each other to boost their flagging totals. But the introduction of Baltic states following the break-up of the Soviet Union really took Eurovision voting bias to a new level.

Estonia triumphed in 2001, aided considerably by twelve points from both Latvia and Lithuania. By contrast, Latvia only managed a total of sixteen points – eight from Estonia and eight from Lithuania. In 2002, it was Latvia's turn, thanks to maximum points from Estonia and Lithuania. Estonia, in return, received twelve points from Latvia and seven from Lithuania. Poor Lithuania received only twelve points, two-thirds of which came from Estonia and Latvia. As well as supporting each other, the trio usually know which side their Baltic bread is buttered and handsomely reward Russia, just in case the latter should be tempted to send in the tanks.

At the 2002 contest in Tallinn, the host nation interspersed the performances with 'postcards', each depicting a fairy tale in a modern Estonian setting. As if that were not excitement enough, in the competition itself Slovenia sent a drag act, Sestre (meaning 'sisters'), whose selection sparked anti-gay protests on the streets of Ljubljana and debate in the Slovenian and European parliaments as to their suitability. The trio – including Damjan Levec, a runner-up at the coveted European Miss Transvestite 1997 – dressed for the show as flight attendants with glittery red suits and skirts, red caps, high heels and lipstick. Let's just say they would never have been mistaken for the Beverley Sisters, although fears have been expressed that their look may have inspired Scooch. Sestre certainly made an impact of sorts and their song, 'Samo Ljubezen' ('Only Love'), finished thirteenth.

There was further controversy when Swedish and Belgian TV commentators advised their viewers not to vote for Israeli singer Sarit Hadad in protest at Israel's treatment of the Palestinians. In the event, she received zero points from Sweden but two from Belgium and finished twelfth overall.

BEWARE GREEKS WEARING LIFTS (2002)

During the twentieth century, Greece was one of the Cinderella countries of Eurovision, its best results being modest fifth place finishes in 1977 and 1992. Throughout that period Greece remained loyal to its roots, generally choosing traditional native music over more westernised pop, regardless of how dated its songs sounded to voters. But in 2002 it bounced into the twenty-first century with a fresh approach. There would be no more introductory lyrics in ancient Greek (1995), or songs about hitch-hiking (1980), clowns (1988) or even Charlie Chaplin (1978). This was Michalis Rakintzis, and he was ready to rock, albeit gingerly.

One of Greece's best-known male singers, Rakintzis was forty-five at the time of the contest, rather advanced in years to be fronting what amounted to a choreographed boy band. They looked like the result of a cross-breeding programme between 911 and the Rolling Stones. For their performance of 'S.A.G.A.P.O.', they wore futuristic black riot gear and heavy boots to appear more imposing. They then stomped around singing about passwords. Anyone tuning in late could have mistaken it for a police raid, except that here the incessant wailing came not from sirens but from the guys on stage. A finishing position of seventeenth said it all.

OFF-KEY IN RIGA (2003)

Many songs are recognisable just from their first couple of notes. Eric Clapton's 'Layla' is one; the moment you hear that opening guitar riff, you know what it is. 'Cry Baby' by Jemini is much the same. As soon as Gemma Abbey opens her mouth, sounding flatter than Holland, you know it is the duo's ill-fated Eurovision performance of 2003. It earned the UK its first-ever *nul points* and was justifiably hailed as the worst vocal exhibition in the contest's history. Not only did she fail to hit the right notes, she didn't even give them a glancing blow.

The sound of Jemini was anything but heavenly. Abbey's agony lasted a full twenty seconds. People have spent less time frantically searching for the right key after locking themselves out of the house. When her partner-in-crime, Chris Cromby, joined in, things settled down a little. At one point, he shouted out, 'Come on!' to the audience in an attempt to get them going. He could consider himself lucky they weren't. By the end it almost sounded as if the pair were singing the same song, but in any case the number itself was no great shakes and the damage had already been done. To add insult to injury, they returned to find that their dressing room had been vandalised. Rumours circulated that music lovers had been responsible.

Cromby later revealed that as each country's votes came in, they had a glass of wine. 'We were tipsy so it was probably a good job we didn't have to go back on to sing.' There was never much danger of that happening.

As the post-mortem began, Gemma Abbey admitted her performance left a little to be desired, but claimed she was unable to hear the backing track due to a technical fault. It later emerged that unlike the other acts, Jemini had not got ear monitors to hear themselves above the backing track. They thought these would be provided automatically. Their manager tried to put a brave face on what fast became a national shame. 'It's a big, big, big pressure event – there's millions of people watching and things can go wrong.' Almost unnecessarily, he added, 'It's not an ideal result.'

The *Daily Mail* reported, 'It was a dog of a song performed by two Scousers who had everything going for them save the fact, harsh but true, that they sang like yowling, cream-curdling banshees.' To show that Jemini held the same appeal across the political spectrum, the *Guardian* described them witheringly as 'a second-rate H and Claire [from Steps] and therefore a third-rate Dollar.'

Terry Wogan had warned before the contest that the UK could expect a voting backlash as a result of the Iraq war and this conspiracy theory was eagerly seized upon by Jemini and their associates. The day after the debacle, Martin Isherwood, the composer of 'Cry Baby', affirmed, 'I think politically we are out on a limb at the moment. As a country, I think we paid the price last night.' The UK's subsequent results certainly tend to suggest that we are not overly popular but the fact remains that it was a lame song and a terrible performance. Even lovely Cheryl Baker, who would have said nice things about Vlad the Impaler, thought it was 'the wrong choice of song' while attributing Gemma's singing to 'nerves'. Louis Walsh, who knows a thing or two about bad acts, was predictably less restrained, branding the song 'a disgrace' and saying Jemini were 'so out of tune they deserved to be last'. Sadly, that summary was, unlike Jemma's voice, not far off the mark.

The impact of the Iraq war on the UK vote was fairly minimal. For even if Jemini had performed 'Cry Baby' while turning Messrs Blair, Bush and Rumsfeld on a medieval torture rack over hot burning coals, they would probably still have finished last.

MIND YOUR LANGUAGE (2003)

Although most Eurovision entries were being performed in English, the language barrier sometimes still presented problems, but Belgium got around this in 2003 by singing in an invented language that nobody could understand. Their song, '*Sanomi*', was performed by six-piece folk band Urban Trad in a totally fictitious tongue, prompting Terry Wogan to remark: 'Three languages to choose from in Belgium, and they had to make up their own!'

The haunting melody may not have meant anything – making it much like any other Eurovision song – but it helped Belgium to finish second. This was its best placing since young Sandra Kim won in 1986 – and just two points behind first-time winners Turkey.

A song that might as well have been sung in a made-up language was Austria's '*Weil Der Mensch Zählt*' ('Man is the Measure of All Things') performed by eccentric comedian Alf Poier in the presence of a series of cardboard cut-outs of farmyard animals. It was intended to be another humorous Austrian send-up of the contest (along the lines of 'Boom Boom Boomerang'), but because Poier sang it in his native Styrian dialect, even standard German speakers would have struggled to make sense of it. Not that there was much sense to be made, for it contained such lines that translated as, 'The difference between people, between apes and primates, it's not much bigger than between noodles and pancake stripes. Pancake stripes.' Quite. The tune veered wildly from simple folk to heavy metal guitars but somehow finished sixth – at the time Austria's best result for over a decade.

RUSSIAN DOLLS (2003)

The majority of Eurovision acts go on a charm offensive in the build-up to the contest so as to garner as much goodwill as possible in the hope that this will translate into votes. Russian duo t.A.T.u. (Yulia Volkova and Lena Katina) gave this practice a subtle twist – they did away with the charm.

The self-styled bad girls of pop began by laying into German entrant Lou, reportedly calling her a witch. They were accused of turning up late for rehearsals and then complained about the stage and the lighting during their press conference, as a result of which they had the unusual experience of being booed by journalists during their own promotion. They so unnerved the European Broadcasting Union that at one point it planned to have a pre-recorded version of the Russian entry ready to substitute during the live broadcast in case the girls got up to any unsuitable lesbian antics on stage. There were also fears that they might perform naked. In the end, these concerns proved unfounded, although they did hold hands and mimic a brief kiss during their performance. There is no firm evidence, however, that their lips actually touched. I should know; I have viewed the incident 107 times.

They made no secret of the fact that they expected to win easily and were installed as the favourites, so it came as a nasty shock when their song, '*Ne Ver', Ne Boisya, Ne Prosi*' ('Don't Believe, Don't Fear, Don't Ask'), finished only third. At this, Russian broadcaster Channel One complained that Ireland had used a backup jury instead of the telephone votes and that this had cost t.A.T.u. victory. Ireland had indeed suffered problems with getting the televote results delivered in time but when they were later released they showed that the Irish public, like the Irish jury, hadn't given t.A.T.u. a single vote. No doubt they all had a good laugh about the misunderstanding back in Moscow.

NOTHING TO CELEBRATE (2004)

To allow more countries to take part, Eurovision introduced a televised semi-final in 2004, and Switzerland marked the occasion with a song and performance so abysmal that it failed to score a single point from the thirty-two voting countries. By scoring *nul points* in a semi-final, the ironically titled 'Celebrate' by Piero Esteriore and the MusicStars became one of the least successful Eurovision songs of all time.

It would not take Sherlock Holmes to see where the problems lay. For a start, clearly more time and money had been spent on the energetic choreography routine than on the song, which was of the singalong type favoured by happy-clappy Christian church bands. Then there was lead singer Piero himself. Not content with accidentally hitting himself in the face with the microphone, he attempted to illustrate his vocal versatility by twice switching from a cheerful chappie to a rock-god growl. Alas, what came out was more George Osborne than Ozzy Osbourne. What really finished them off, however, was the big dance break part-way through. Until then, Piero's four backing artists had done their best to conceal his vocal inadequacies but when they returned to microphone duties after bouncing around the stage they were so breathless that only the sounds of strained wheezing could be heard. Nobody seemed to have factored this into the equation.

Piero battled on gamely, urging us to celebrate, but his heart was no longer in it; he must have feared that paramedics were about to rush on at any minute and cart away his entire backing band on stretchers. As half-word followed half-word and the unscripted panting became almost obscene, the end could not come soon enough. Rarely has a score of zero been so thoroughly merited.

BREAKING THE ICE (2004)

As the unlikely hosts of the 2004 Eurovision Song Contest, Turkey clearly decided that it should behave graciously towards all its guests, even those it had clashed with in the past.

Turkey and Cyprus had ignored each other voting-wise for over twenty years so it came as a huge surprise when, in 2003, for the first time, Cyprus had awarded points to a Turkish song. The Cypriot gift of eight points – an event that had once seemed about as likely as Cain and Abel sending each other birthday cards – made all the difference and enabled Turkey to claim its first victory. Cyprus gave Turkey four points in 2004, whereupon Turkey reciprocated the gesture by awarding the Cypriot entry five points – the first time that Turkey had ever awarded Cyprus a single vote. But Turkey couldn't resist having one little dig.

When each country announced its votes, an outline map of that country appeared on screen – except in the case of Cyprus. Instead Turkish broadcaster TRT refused to display a map of the island to avoid highlighting the ongoing dispute over the northern half, which Turkey recognises as an independent republic. Even so, it was all a step in the right direction.

TRT also upset Slovenia in the semi-final by accidentally going to a commercial break just as the Slovenian entry, 'Stay Forever' by

Platin, was about to be performed. As Turkish viewers were not able to see or hear the song they didn't give it any votes. They shouldn't feel too bad about it, though, because the rest of Europe did see and hear the Slovenian song and they hardly gave it any votes either.

Ultimately, the 2004 contest produced another new winner, Ukraine. The victorious singer, Ruslana, was presented with the trophy by the previous year's winner, Sertab Erener, but only after Erener, about to step on stage for the ceremony, got her shoe stuck in a speaker grill and had to be freed by stagehands.

JAVINE'S BOOB (2005)

As a glamour model, reality TV star and best-selling author, Katie Price (aka Jordan) was already spreading her limited talents precariously thin, so to embark on a singing career was decidedly bold – particularly given the fact that she couldn't actually sing. However, one thing her detractors could never accuse her of is being publicity-shy, so it was entirely in character when she put herself forward as the UK's prospective 2005 Eurovision representative. No previous experience or singing ability required. Must be confident and be free the third weekend in May. She fitted the bill perfectly.

Armed with a totally forgettable song, 'Not Just Anybody', she decided to perform on the BBC's selection show, *Making Your Mind Up* (the new version of *A Song for Europe*), in an outfit that she hoped would appeal to her fans – a skin-tight, pink latex catsuit. Heavily made up and tanned, she was anything but a vision in pink and instead looked like Barbie on the game. She appeared decidedly ill at ease on stage – like someone who had stepped too far out of her comfort zone – and moved slowly and awkwardly with the style and grace of a *Thunderbirds* puppet. Her mobility was not helped by the fact that she was six months' pregnant.

Although she started as clear favourite by virtue of having the highest celebrity profile, Price was beaten into second place by Javine, a reject from reality TV show *Popstars: The Rivals*. Javine achieved the near-impossible by managing to upstage her rival when her skimpy dress slipped briefly during her energetic encore rendition of 'Touch My Fire' to create what is euphemistically known as a 'wardrobe malfunction'. Ironically, Price had kept her assets covered up for once. Javine denied that the dress debacle had been staged and put it down to the excitement of the moment. 'I had just been told I'd won,' she trilled, 'and I was jumping up and down and hugging everyone. The tape came away from my dress and it popped out. It's one of those little things that happens during live TV.'

Javine did not have long to bask in the glory. She went on to represent the UK in the final in Kiev, where, apparently suffering from a throat infection, she finished twenty-second, ahead of only France and Germany.

Katie Price has led a roller-coaster life and claims to have few regrets – but says one was entering Eurovision. She confessed in a 2015 interview, 'I looked shocking, I sounded shocking and I couldn't sing the song now. In fact, I couldn't sing it then!' We could have told her all that at the time.

THE DRUMMING GRANDMA (2005)

Moldova made its Eurovision debut in 2005 and immediately introduced the rest of Europe to a new rock phenomenon – the drumming grandma. The Moldovan entry, '*Boonika Bate Doba*' ('Grandma Beats the Drum'), was performed partly in English and partly in Romanian by Zdob și Zdub. They were a lively, colourfully-attired bunch whose name is onomatopoeic for the sound of a drum beat and whose star turn was a grandma banging a big bass drum while reclining in a rocking chair. Towards the end, she even got out of her chair for a show-stopping solo spot. For all I know about the Moldovan rock scene, maybe every band out there has a drumming grandparent as part of a scheme to provide employment for the elderly. We may mock, but is it really so different from Rolling Stones' sticksman Charlie Watts?

The band went a step further for the song's video, in which grandmothers from various countries were shown playing the drum around the world.

This was a long way removed from the dreary plastic pop submitted by the UK and '*Boonika Bate Doba*' came second in the semi-final. It went on to finish a creditable sixth in the final, picking up 130 more points than Javine. Demonstrating that it was never slow to catch on to a gimmick, five years later the UK wheeled out seventy-six-year-old Engelbert Humperdinck.

PRAISE THE LORDI (2006)

With such a diversity of cultures in Europe, it is never easy trying to predict what type of song will go down well and which will sink without trace before you can say Andy Abraham.

A group of Finns of indeterminate ages playing ear-piercing heavy metal while wearing grotesque latex horror masks and monster costumes in front of a backdrop of spectacular pyrotechnics was a far cry from Dana's 'All Kinds of Everything', but Lordi's 'Hard Rock Hallelujah' turned out to be one of the most popular – and certainly most recognisable – winners of the twenty-first century. It also gave Finland its first Eurovision success, at the fortieth attempt.

The *Daily Telegraph* wrote, 'Lordi's studded-leather costumes, blood-spurting chainsaws and spine-tingling lyrics left the traditional spangle-suited, love-ballad-singing entrants strewn around the Olympic stadium in Athens like extras in a zombie film.' It was the year when Eurovision viewers finally got tired of sequins.

Quite simply, Lordi, a death metal band whose motto was 'Europe get ready to get scared', were not what you expected to see at a Eurovision Song Contest. It was like someone hiring Iron Maiden to play at a vicar's tea party or getting Ozzy Osbourne to make the National Lottery draw.

'Hard Rock Hallelujah' was written by lead singer Mr Lordi who, after storming the semi-final, declared that the only changes the band would make for the final would be 'to scream louder and turn the amps up'. To homes still accustomed to nothing raunchier and sweatier than the latest Euro-pop moppet, this must have sounded more of a threat than a promise. Embellishing his performance with a two-headed battleaxe and bat-like wings, Mr Lordi and his cohorts, who had names like OX and Amen, blasted away the opposition once more, beating Russia into second place. This time, the Russians did not object. Even they knew better than to mess with Lordi.

A NOT VERY SUBLIMINAL
MESSAGE (2006)

Lithuania was not happy. The advent of Baltic bloc voting had already produced wins for Estonia and Latvia but they had seemingly missed the boat. With more and more countries being admitted to the contest every year, by 2006 Lithuania could have been forgiven for fearing that it was drinking in the last chance saloon. So for that year's contest in Athens, it tried to brainwash voters by sending six-piece band LT United to perform the football-like chant 'We Are The Winners', a repetitive anthem proclaiming Lithuania to be the winners of the Eurovision Song Contest. It was wishful thinking on a grand scale.

'We are the winners of Eurovision,' ran the lyrics, 'so vote, vote, vote for the winners.' As a message, it was only slightly less subliminal than being repeatedly beaten over the head with a blunt instrument. The band were dressed like a team of middle managers who had just stepped out of an oh-so-important meeting about quarterly projections, but appearances can be deceptive for, as Terry Wogan warned, 'Keep an eye out for a bald maniac who may be Harry Hill's brother.' The bald maniac did not disappoint, bursting into a sudden dance routine that would have caused havoc on the floor of the Vilnius presidential palace. The performance was booed at the end by some of the Greek audience, who presumably objected to the overconfident sentiments of the song. It is difficult to imagine Lithuania having offended Greece in any other way. Taken literally, the message failed because 'We Are The Winners' finished only sixth in the final, but this easily represented Lithuania's best result to date. At the after-show press conference Lordi, the real winners, sang a chorus of it as they entered. For LT United, it was a sort of reflected glory.

Latvia did its best to leave the way clear for its neighbour by sending six-piece a cappella group Cosmos to sing 'I Hear Your Heart'. They were joined on stage by a small robot that danced with them in the final chorus. It was all very low-tech and would only have been likely to have the same impact as Lordi if the rockers had turned up with just a single sparkler for their pyrotechnics. Latvia finished only sixteenth. It obviously had no ambitions to host the event in 2007.

BACK TO SCHOOL (2006)

As befits his name, Daz Sampson is whiter than white, which is rarely a good thing for a rap artist. To make matters worse, Stockport's answer to Eminem was a thirty-one-year-old white rapper surrounded by four backing singers dressed as schoolgirls. It is best not to speculate which section of the community they were hoping to appeal to with those costumes but the overall impression given by the UK entry at the 2006 Eurovision was somewhere between creepy and pervy. The voters were certainly not captivated by Daz and his Sampsonites (as the schoolgirls were nicknamed) and put their song, 'Teenage Life', in nineteenth place, with only ten of the thirty-nine eligible countries awarding it any points at all. That was a shame, because the song, which Sampson co-wrote, wasn't bad.

Afterwards Sampson claimed that his performance may have raised the popularity of the contest in the UK as the show attracted particularly high viewing figures that year. 'It was like I was taking Eurovision back to the common man,' he said, 'and viewing figures reflected that.' Or it could be that people watched him for the same reason they gawp at car crashes on motorways. He then generously offered his services to the nation once more, saying he would like to try for the 2007

Eurovision. The BBC diplomatically told him that it was probably a bit too soon. They would let him know when the time was right. He's still waiting.

THE WRONG WINNER (2007)

Throughout his long and distinguished career, you could count the number of slip-ups Terry Wogan made on the fingers of Captain Hook's hands. There was no more risk of Wogan making an embarrassing on-air blunder than . . . oh, I don't know – of a bearded lady winning the Eurovision Song Contest. Yet when it came to announcing the results of the BBC's 2007 *Making Your Mind Up*, he committed the cardinal sin of declaring the wrong winner.

The selection contest boiled down to a sing-off between two acts, Scooch and Cyndi and – following the statutory prolonged pause which has become the norm for such world-shattering declarations – Wogan and co-presenter Fearne Cotton announced the result in dramatic unison. But whereas she said, 'Scooch', he said, 'Cyndi'. It was as if the front two legs of a pantomime horse had gone to the right and the back two had gone to the left.

Standing beside the presenters on stage, both acts looked suitably baffled, whereupon Cotton quickly corrected Wogan and, after a few seconds of confusion, Cyndi's joy evaporated as Scooch were now confirmed as the winners by 53 per cent of the votes to 47 per cent. 'It's Scooch, it's Scooch,' the pair proclaimed, finally finding common ground. It was left to Cotton to console poor Cyndi.

The BBC insisted that Wogan had been given the right name in his earpiece, but pointed out that the studio was very noisy at the time. It was a mess, a right royal Eurovision mess, but as Sir Terry later said on his radio show, 'Nobody died, it's a TV programme.'

CRASH-LANDING (2007)

Looking back, it could be that Wogan's announcement of Cyndi as the UK's representative in Helsinki was not a faux-pas as such but simply the result of him dreaming aloud. For then we all would have been spared the sheer embarrassment of Scooch. Welsh singer Charlotte Church has not always been on the same wavelength as the rest of the UK but she spoke for many when she described Scooch's song as 'absolute shit'. This prompted band member Russ Spencer to reply, 'What a pity the voice of an angel has acquired the mouth of a sewer.' That quote was arguably the highlight of Scooch's career.

For their performance of 'Flying The Flag (For You)', Scooch dressed up as flight attendants. Natalie Powers and Caroline Barnes were 'trolley dollies' while the two men, Spencer and David Ducasse, camped it up in a manner reminiscent of Mr Humphries in *Are You Being Served?*. Their flight had travelled thirty years back in time. It was all horribly dated, complete with sexual innuendo including '. . . and *blow* into the mouthpiece', and 'would you like something to suck on for landing, sir?' In fact, the whole thing sucked – it could have been a scene from *Carry On Flying*. It almost made viewers feel nostalgic for Jemini.

We were offered brief hope when a Swedish singer, Pandora, claimed that the chorus of 'Flying The Flag' was a blatant copy of a song she had released in 1999 and demanded that it be disqualified from taking part in Eurovision. Alas, she was unsuccessful. The BBC confirmed that 'Flying The Flag' was original. It was crap, but it was original crap.

Thinking that Scooch was what passed for twenty-first-century humour in Britain, the voters of Europe awarded the song just nineteen points, leaving it languishing in twenty-second place, 249 points behind winners Serbia. A dozen of Scooch's points came from Malta – the UK's first maximum for five years – but far from being a vindication of the song, it turned out they were nothing more than a protest vote. The points were given to the UK because Malta was fed up with the way every other country voted for its neighbours. The UK's other seven points came from Ireland, its . . . er, neighbour.

Condemnation of Scooch and the song was swift and merciless. The *Sunday Mirror* said the 'cheesy quartet' had made us 'the laughing stock of Europe', while The *Sunday Times* called it 'a crash-landing'. Ex-Darkness frontman Justin Hawkins, who lost out to Scooch in *Making Your Mind Up*, gained a modicum of revenge by stating, 'The BBC shouldn't have put it forward. It was supposed to be different this year. The clue is in the title, Eurovision Song Contest. It should have been a song.' Former Radio 1 DJ Mike Read described the choreography as 'appalling', which was actually being kind, and added, 'If that is the best that this country, full of great songwriters, can come up with, then heaven help us!'

Meanwhile, somewhere out there Cyndi was having a wry smile to herself.

BALKAN CARVE-UP (2007)

The widespread bloc voting that prevailed in the Eurovision Song Contest was only partly to blame for the UK's woeful results in the noughties, but it was in danger of turning the whole event into an even bigger farce than it was already. In addition to the Baltic bloc, we now had the eastern European bloc and the Balkan bloc (not to mention the traditional Scandinavian bias), so that by 2007 it had reached the stage where viewers could accurately predict to which song a particular country's votes would be awarded before the spokesperson had even opened his or her mouth. You didn't need an ear for a good song; all you needed was a map. This was more than just loving thy neighbour; this was shagging her senseless.

In Helsinki that year, Belarus got twelve from Ukraine and Russia; Russia got twelve from Armenia, Belarus and Estonia; Romania got twelve from Moldova; Moldova got twelve from Romania; Finland got twelve from Sweden and Iceland; Sweden got twelve from Denmark and Norway.

Not all of these generous gifts could be reciprocated because some countries (Iceland, Denmark, Norway and Estonia) were not actually in the final, having been eliminated in the semi-final. They were still eligible to vote.

However, the biggest winner was Serbia, whose song '*Molitva*' ('Prayer'), an unexceptional power ballad though undeniably well performed, won with the help of twelve points from neighbours Montenegro, Bosnia-Herzegovina, Croatia, Slovenia and Macedonia. Interestingly none of these countries gave Ukraine, Serbia's closest rival, more than five points.

The voting patterns caused such consternation in parts of western Europe that Liberal Democrat MP Richard Younger-Ross tabled a motion in the UK parliament, signed by three other MPs, 'That this House believes that voting in the Eurovision Song Contest has become a joke as countries vote largely on narrow nationalistic grounds or for neighbour countries rather than the quality of the song; and that such narrow voting is harmful to the relationship between the peoples of Europe; and calls for the BBC to insist on changes to the voting system or to withdraw from the contest.'

While valid, his argument might have carried more weight had our entry not been Scooch.

A UKRAINIAN NOVELTY (2007)

If Scooch needed reminding that a novelty act could do well at Eurovision with a decent song, they needed to look no further than the runner-up in Helsinki, 'Dancing *Lasha Tumbai*'.

Ukrainian drag character Verka Serduchka (played by comedian Andriy Mykhailovych Danylko), took to the stage in a shiny silver outfit that was described by one observer as 'an oven-ready

Christopher Biggins'. He and his similarly attired dancers proceeded to raise the roof with a spirited dance routine that might have proved a bit too much for Biggins, even as Widow Twankey.

To enhance its international appeal, the song had lyrics in four languages – Ukrainian, German, Russian and English – and had the distinction of being one of the few to be enhanced by the presence of an accordion. Ukrainian nationalists and members of the country's parliament had vociferously expressed their disapproval at the selection of Serduchka on the grounds that the character – a cult figure in the country – is 'vulgar and offensive' and 'a grotesque stereotype of a middle-aged woman'. Back in the 1960s, there were some elderly spinsters in the Shetlands who said much the same about Kenneth McKellar.

DUSTIN THE TURKEY (2008)

In 2008, having not won the Eurovision for twelve years and having finished last the previous year, Ireland came up with a new strategy: it would dispense with human performers and select a glove puppet instead. So it was that Dustin the Turkey earned his place in Eurovision history. The logic was sound, for although no puppet had ever won Eurovision, plenty of turkeys had.

Operated by John Morrison, Dustin, who to be biologically accurate is half-turkey, half-vulture, made his debut on RTE's afternoon kids' show *The Den* in a 1990 guest appearance alongside the show's anarchic stars, Zig and Zag, who were co-created by Morrison's eldest brother Ciaran. When Zig and Zag left to pursue fame in the UK on Channel 4's *The Big Breakfast*, Dustin seized his opportunity. He was given his own show, *Dustin's Daily News*, stood in a political election as a Fianna Fowl candidate and demonstrated his singing prowess by releasing fourteen singles and six albums that regularly topped the Irish charts at Christmas. He was therefore the only turkey who actively looked forward to the festive season. In 1996, he reportedly outsold Boyzone and Daniel O'Donnell to finish the year as Ireland's top-selling artist. His 2005 album, *Bling When You're Minging*, even featured a duet with Chris de Burgh.

Then in 2008, the bird with a penchant for burping was plucked from a line-up of six finalists in Limerick to represent Ireland in that year's Eurovision with his gobbled rendition of '*Irelande Douze Pointe*'. The song, composed by Darren Smith and Simon Fine, pleaded, 'Give us another chance, we're sorry for *Riverdance*,' adding, 'Eastern Europe we love you, do you like Irish stew or goulash as it is to you?' The chorus urged the audience to 'Shake your feathers and bop your beak, shake 'em to the west and to the east, wave Euro hands and Euro feet, wave 'em in the air to the turkey beat.' On a note of graver national importance, the lyrics also referred to Sir Terry Wogan's (alleged) wig.

Dustin performed his entry surrounded by a group of feathered dancers, perched on top of a shopping cart. When it was announced that he had won, there were audible boos from the

Irish audience and Dana went so far as to state that Ireland would be better withdrawing from the contest than sending Dustin. The turkey was confident, however. 'This isn't even a song; it's an anthem, a hymn,' he claimed. 'It's uniting Europe. I want to reach out my wings and say we're all one, we're all friends. Well, besides the Poles – I don't really like them.'

Sadly for Dustin that was the year when the Eurovision introduced two semi-finals to the programme. He finished fifteenth out of nineteen countries in his Belgrade semi, picking up just twenty-two points – 134 behind winners Greece – and was eliminated. He had thus been deprived of his big night on the main Eurovision stage. Dustin the Turkey had been well and truly stuffed.

Reflecting on Dustin's failure, the *Irish Examiner* wrote that the song 'is now set to take its rightful place in the annals of Euro songs which only the drunk, demented or both will add to their Christmas party repertoire'.

SHIVER ME TIMBERS (2008)

Eurovision performances have become increasingly visual with each passing year. When the contest began back in the 1950s, singers would stand almost motionless at the microphone, the only concession to choreography being the occasional wave of an arm or a nervous tic. Many now go in for spectacular productions and outlandish costumes.

Latvia's Swedish-written 2008 entry, 'Wolves of the Sea', was performed by a band called Pirates of the Sea, who, naturally enough, raided the fancy-dress box and donned pirate costumes. They put on a suitably swashbuckling show, boasting about how they were going to raid the high seas, plundering and murdering, 'With a hi-hi-ho'. It would appear that Snow White had gone rogue.

Collecting twelve points from Ireland and ten from the UK, 'Wolves of the Sea' finished twelfth in Belgrade and achieved a significant afterlife (something relatively few losing Eurovision songs manage) when it was adopted as an anthem for the South African national rugby team, the Springboks.

ANGELS AND DEMONS (2008)

Azerbaijan certainly did not hold back on its Eurovision debut.
It wasn't going to ease itself into the fray with a traditional folk song about a mountain goatherd – instead it sent male duo Elnur and Samir to Belgrade to perform 'Day After Day', a crazily over-the-top number that mixed opera and rock and featured dancers dressed as demons and angels. It was Guns N' Roses meets the Nolans. With its bursts of falsetto and mangled words, you could watch it a dozen times and still not make much sense of it (even though it was sung in English) except for deducing from the costumes that it had something to do with the eternal battle between good and evil. Having said that, it deserved to finish as high as eighth, seventeen places above the UK entry sung by Andy Abraham. It's good to know that in Eurovision terms, we're a third-rate Azerbaijan. Pointless Eurovision fact: Elnur (Hüseynov) of Elnur and Samir has a degree in dentistry.

GEORGIA ON THEIR MIND (2009)

Most of the excitement surrounding the 2009 Eurovision took place long before the actual contest. First came the bombshell that Sir Terry Wogan had finally decided to step down as UK commentator. Although he admitted to being peeved by the unfairness of the partisan voting, he acknowledged that for all its faults he had enjoyed 'the silly songs, the spectacle, the grandiose foolishness of it all'. To replace the seemingly irreplaceable, the BBC wanted one of its biggest stars, but Nick Knowles was busy so the corporation settled on Graham Norton, who quickly put his own quirky stamp on the annual bash.

One country that Norton did not have to worry about for his first Eurovision broadcast was Georgia. Having made its debut in 2007, Georgia planned to enter a 1970s-inspired disco-funk number for 2009 by Stephane & 3G titled 'We Don't Wanna Put In'. It was chosen by public vote and jury (the combination of televoting and five-member juries was introduced across Eurovision-land in 2009 to determine the number of votes cast for each entry), but the song's lyrics attracted controversy as they appeared to be taking a barely concealed pop at Russian leader Vladimir Putin.

The chorus ran: 'We don't wanna put in, the negative move, it's killing the groove. I'm gonna try to shoot in, some disco tonight. Boogie with you.' Did Georgia really think it could get away with that, especially as the two countries had gone to war only the previous year?

The Georgian Public Broadcaster maintained that the lyrics were perfectly innocent, but the European Broadcasting Union ruled that they breached rules which forbid political comment. Sensitive to the fact that the final was being staged in Moscow, the EBU demanded that either the words were changed or Georgia should pick another song. Georgia withdrew from the contest.

Another to pull out, as opposed to put in, was Rita Ora who, as a sixteen-year-old, auditioned that year in front of Lord Andrew Lloyd Webber to be the UK contestant but left before hearing whether she was the chosen one. 'Right from the start, I was like, "What am I doing here?",' she said four years later with three UK No. 1s under her belt. 'I did my song and walked out. They started looking for me, calling my agent. Imagine if I'd stayed. It would probably be all over for me. At best, I'd be a contestant on that diving show, *Splash!*' The 2009 UK selection competition was eventually won by Jade Ewen. Just a couple of months before Ora's comments, Ewen appeared on *Splash!* Miaow!

A GIMMICK TOO FAR (2010)

Having failed with the subliminal message approach, Lithuania tried the Bucks Fizz trick in 2010. The trouble was, nobody seemed to have told band InCulto that the business of whipping away items of clothing to reveal shapely legs works much better with women than it does with five blokes, especially five blokes who looked like accountants. Thus when the quintet made a great show of pulling away their checked trousers – the sort favoured by Rupert Bear – to reveal glittery silver hot pants, the effect was not dissimilar to five embarrassing uncles dancing at a wedding. You can't help suspecting that one of them had recently seen *The Full Monty*. That film has a lot to answer for.

Lithuania had previously considered withdrawing from the 2010 contest due to the escalating cost, until private funding enabled InCulto and Lithuania to go to the ball. Frankly, the company that put up the cash would have been better off investing in chocolate teapots.

InCulto were formed by Jurgis Didžiulis (whose wife, Erica Jennings, had represented Lithuania with SKAMP in the 2001 contest) and their song, 'Eastern European Funk', blended rhythms of his Colombian childhood with Lithuanian folk music. At least, that's what it said on the tin. However, the subtle South

American aromas made no greater impact on the voters of Europe than did the sparkly hot pants and InCulto were booted off the Eurovision process at the semi-final stage after finishing only twelfth. They broke up less than a year later. We all have to live with the loss.

AN UNINVITED GUEST (2010)

Ever since Denmark held the 2001 Eurovision in a football stadium with a capacity of thirty-eight thousand (compared to the two thousand capacity of Dublin's Gaiety theatre in 1971), the contest had been getting bigger and more expensive. So when Norway found itself obliged to stage the 2010 event, cash-strapped national broadcaster NRK raised the estimated twenty million pounds by selling its broadcast rights to that year's World Cup to a rival. It was all worth it and the NRK bubbly flowed again in Oslo on the night of 29 May – because the Norwegian song finished a lowly twentieth, sparing the broadcaster the financial burden of staging the contest in 2011. Not since Ireland in the mid-1990s had Eurovision failure been the cause of such celebration.

The organisers might perhaps have spent a few more kroner on security in Oslo. There was a one-man stage invasion during the Spanish entry in the final. Second in the running order, Daniel Diges was part-way through his performance of '*Algo Pequeñito*' ('Something Tiny') when serial Catalan football pitch-invader Jaume Marquet Cot (aka Jimmy Jump), climbed on to the stage purely in the interest of self-promotion and joined the four dancers in their marionette-inspired dance routine. He remained on stage for over twenty seconds before security personnel finally appeared and he disappeared back into the audience. Diges gamely carried on singing throughout the interruption, but was allowed to perform the song again at the end. He finished fifteenth, which, if nothing else, was ten places higher than Josh Dubovie, who ensured that the UK finished last for the third time in eight years; this from a country that had only twice finished outside the Top 10 until 1999.

Dubovie's song, co-written by Pete Waterman, was titled 'That Sounds Good to Me'. Not to anyone else it didn't. Described as bearing all the hallmarks of an old Rick Astley song (this was not a compliment) and slated by *Times Online* for being 'the pop equivalent of reprocessed meat', it reached no higher than No. 179 in the UK singles chart, surprising a lot of people who didn't know the chart went down that low. Indeed, some suspect it was extended solely to cater for our Eurovision entries.

HURRICANE JEDWARD
HITS EUROVISION (2011)

Troublesome things often come in pairs – earthquake and after-shock, thunder and lightning, drunk and disorderly. To this list can be added Jedward. With relentless energy and self-confidence that seems impervious to all criticism – 'irritating', 'talentless' and 'vile little creatures' are among the kinder comments that have been thrown at them – the brothers Grimes (not to be confused with the Brothers Grimm who are much less scary) are the quintessential Eurovision act. They first shot to fame on that showcase of the quickly forgotten, *The X Factor*, but have managed to buck the trend, albeit in an ironic kind of way. To this day it is hard to know whether they are in on the joke or whether they really believe they are good.

David Cameron once claimed he was 'addicted' to Jedward and reportedly bought a T-shirt with their faces on it. Mind you, there was a general election to win at the time. Thinking about it, the twins are addictive – in the same way as Maltesers. For just as too many Maltesers can make you feel sick, more than two minutes of Jedward has a similar effect. They are just so hyper, like a pair of untrained puppies. One interviewer described chatting to them as like being mown down by a juggernaut. Their trademark gravity-defying hair suggests that they have just had a thousand volts passed through their bodies in electric chairs. Coincidentally, putting Jedward in electric chairs is believed to be high on the wish list of several music critics.

The twins performed 'Lipstick' for Ireland at the 2011 Eurovision in Germany and, after battling through the semi-final, finished a respectable eighth in the final, unsurprisingly earning twelve points from the UK. In Australia's separate TV voting, 'Lipstick' was named the most popular song. It was enough to encourage them to try again the following year when, hair flattened and in silver costumes that could have been loaned by the Tin Man from *The Wizard Of Oz*, they jumped and ran around the stage even more manically than usual. Any synchronised choreography was purely coincidental. However, maybe the previous year's novelty had worn off on the voters of Europe because this time their song, 'Waterline', came only nineteenth in the final. The ten points they received from the UK made up almost a quarter of their total vote.

That Eurovision performance ended with them getting soaked under a fountain and many people can't wait for their career to go the same way – down the plughole. Indeed, a number of music forums have been dedicated to the simple notion that the twins are crap, their demise is long overdue and Jedward will soon be deadwood. True, they are as annoying as that bluebottle which buzzes incessantly and tunelessly around the room on a summer's day that you just can't get rid of but you have to admire their skill at selling themselves. It may take more than a rolled-up newspaper to bring about their downfall.

RETURN OF THE PUNK FAIRIES (2011)

If you had woken suddenly during the Moldovan entry at the 2011 Eurovision Song Contest to see flashing red, green and yellow lights and a group of strange men in tall pointy hats rocking out next to a trumpet-playing fairy riding a unicycle, you could be forgiven for blaming it on a bad drugs experience or at the very least too much cheese. Instead, it was our old friends Zdob și Zdub, heroes of 2005, but this time without their drumming grandma.

Here they were representing their country for a second time at Eurovision, on this occasion with 'So Lucky' and giving a typically eccentric performance which one reviewer described as 'mad as a box of frogs'. As pioneers of the punk fairy movement, their stage act in Düsseldorf was an intriguing mix of *Alice in Wonderland* and the Damned. Think the Mad Hatter meets Damned drummer Rat Scabies and you'll get the general idea. It was the very essence of Eurovision and deserved to finish higher than twelfth.

The 2011 semi-finals had witnessed the return of another Eurovision icon, Dana International, who represented Israel thirteen years on from her famous triumph with the self-penned 'Ding Dong'. Alas, this was not a tribute to Leslie Phillips but a rather weak disco offering which owed more to Kelly Marie than Donna Summer. Still, Dana Int. must have thought that with such a Eurovision-friendly title and her own presence, she would sweep through to the final. In the end, she finished only fifteenth out of nineteen, thus becoming the first former winner to be knocked out in the semi-finals.

With the exception of Johnny Logan, past winners rarely seem to do well at Eurovision. Sweden's Charlotte Nilsson won in 1999 but, as Charlotte Perrelli, could only finish eighteenth in 2008 while Ireland's Niamh Kavanagh, the winner in 1993, managed no higher than twenty-third on her return in 2010. Their motto should be: if at first you do succeed, don't push your luck by trying again.

THE RUSSIAN GRANDMOTHERS (2012)

Moldova may have dispensed with its Eurovision grandma for 2012, but Russia introduced half a dozen of them as *Buranovskiye Babushki* **(The Grannies from Buranovo).** They were like a Spice Girls in which every member was Old Spice.

This group of groovy grannies, the oldest of whom was seventy-six, hailed from a remote Russian village in Udmurtia and took the contest by storm with their rousing rendition of 'Party for Everybody', which eventually finished second behind Sweden, receiving votes from forty out of the forty-one eligible countries. Switzerland was the only party-pooper. Wearing traditional dresses, they shuffled across the stage while belting out their hard-partying anthem with its English chorus: 'Party for every-body – dance! Come on and dance! Come on and dance! Come on and boom boom . . . We wanna boom, boom, boom, we wanna party-party. We wanna boom, boom, boom for everybody.' Great for Eurovision, but the sort of behaviour that is sometimes frowned upon in a retirement home.

The group had been discovered singing locally in 2008 and first tried to enter Eurovision two years later with a song titled 'How to Make Birch Bark into a Hat'. For some unaccountable reason the Russian public failed to see the merit in a musical arts and crafts demonstration and the song was not selected. After that, they realised they needed to be a little more rock 'n' roll.

Should their Eurovision routine have encouraged you to want to listen to their back catalogue, you might like to know that they have recorded cover versions of 'Let It Be', 'Hotel California', 'We Are the Champions' and Deep Purple's 'Smoke on the Water', all sung in their local dialect of Udmurt. Refreshingly, the money they make from sales does not go on funding a cocaine or knitting habit but is put towards the rebuilding of their village church.

ANKE PUTS THE BOOT IN (2012)

Following Ell & Nikki's success in 2011 with 'Running Scared', Baku, the capital of Azerbaijan, was the venue for the 2012 Eurovision but it proved highly controversial. In the run-up to the event, Iran condemned Azerbaijan for 'anti-Islamic behaviour', claiming that by staging the contest it was effectively hosting a 'gay parade'. This led to protests in front of the Iranian embassy in Baku and when Iran was told to mind its own business, it recalled its ambassador. Azerbaijan demanded an apology over Iran's comments and when none was forthcoming, it recalled its own ambassador from Tehran.

Azerbaijan came under fire from many quarters over its poor human rights record but no criticism was delivered with such charm as by German presenter Anke Engelke. Appearing live on screen to deliver her country's votes in the final, she gave a beaming smile and a happy wave and, as is the custom on these occasions, began by congratulating Azerbaijan on putting on such a wonderful show. Then, without changing the tone of her voice or losing her cheery demeanour, she continued, 'Tonight nobody could vote for their own country. But it is good to be able to vote. And it is good to have a choice. Good luck on your journey, Azerbaijan. Europe is watching you. And here are the results of the German jury . . .' All that the Azerbaijani hosts could do was smile back in return, through gritted teeth.

YOUR BUM HAS FEELINGS (2012)

One song that failed to make it through to the 2012 final was San Marino's 'The Social Network Song' sung by Valentina Monetta. It was originally titled 'Facebook Uh, Oh, Oh' but mention of the company name contravened Eurovision rules regarding product placement. Maybe it wasn't worth the effort since one critic described it as 'the most cringeworthy Eurovision song in many years'. This was rather unfair because the lyrics are clearly a satirical swipe at the power of social media and how friendships can be acquired at the click of a mouse. Although Ms Monetta made the effort by dressing from head to toe in blue leather, the tune was unremarkable and it finished only fourteenth in its semi-final.

It was a shame nobody was forced to alter the lyrics of another semi-final casualty, the Austrian entry '*Woki mit deim Popo*' ('Waggle your Bum') by male hip-hop duo Trackshittaz. Thankfully, it was performed in Mühlviertlerisch, an obscure dialect spoken only in Upper Austria, thus making it unintelligible to most of Europe. Translated into English its lines included, 'Your bum has feelings, your bum is a part of you. Don't put it on chairs, your bum has an opinion, yeah.' It must have left Bernie Taupin tearing Elton's hair out. Trackshittaz's routine was marked by screams from the audience, which either meant they had a few fans or more likely that a rat had been spotted in the hall. Although their performance made clever use of lighting, it earned a meagre eight points, giving it the lowest score of any semi-finalist that year. They were not greatly missed at the final.

WHERE ARE THE POINTS
WE PAID FOR? (2013)

The 2013 Eurovision in Malmö, Sweden, was marred by allegations of vote rigging and attempted bribery, with most of the accusations surrounding Azerbaijan. On the day of the final, a Lithuanian media outlet released an undercover video suggesting that representatives from Azerbaijan were trying to bribe Lithuanian students in return for multiple votes. The EBU subsequently launched an investigation that concluded there had been an unsuccessful attempt at cheating but that it was not linked to the official Azerbaijani delegation.

There was more bad feeling when Azerbaijan officially awarded no points to Dina Garipova of Russia even though she had reportedly come second in the country's phone poll. Not for the first time Russia protested, claiming that the Azerbaijani vote had been falsified. Russian foreign minister Sergei Lavrov said the points had been 'stolen' from Russia and warned, 'This outrageous action will not remain without a response.' The Russians were particularly aggrieved as they had awarded Azerbaijan's Farid Mammadov the maximum twelve points, helping him to finish a surprisingly high second behind Denmark. Russia came fifth.

Meanwhile, Belarus, having received no points from Russia, saw that as an opportunity to accuse the Russians of skulduggery. The Eurovision record of Belarus at that time showed that it had awarded twice as many points to Russia as to any other country, so it was not happy at receiving zilch in return. Suddenly any country that received no points viewed it as the basis to launch a claim of cheating. Jahn Teigen could have kept lawyers busy for years.

That there might be some truth to these allegations became more likely when the UK entrant, Bonnie Tyler, who described the voting as 'unbelievable' after being placed nineteenth, told a French newspaper she had overheard Russians complaining that Azerbaijan did not 'give us the ten points we paid for'. Potentially damning evidence unless, of course, the true translation of her comments was lost in France.

At sixty-one, Bonnie Tyler was a surprising choice (after the Josh Dubovie flop, the BBC selected the artist internally) as her last big hit had come nearly a decade before the winner, Denmark's Emmelie de Forest, was born. Tyler was said to be reluctant to take part initially, perhaps because she knew she couldn't use her bus pass abroad. But at least she represented progress on the 2012 choice, Engelbert Humperdinck, who last had a UK hit when Graham Norton was still at school. For 2014, the BBC were rumoured to be checking Wikipedia to see if Pearl Carr and Teddy Johnson were still alive.

FINLAND'S SAME-SEX KISS (2013)

Ever since t.A.T.u. had held hands back in 2003, the Eurovision Song Contest had been waiting for its first full-blown, same-sex kiss. It duly arrived when, at the end of her song 'Marry Me', Finland's Krista Siegfrids locked lips with one of her female backing singers in a move that was designed to encourage Finland to legalise same-sex marriage. Predictably, some countries – notably Turkey and Greece – reacted negatively to the kiss, protesting that it broke Eurovision rules forbidding 'gestures of a political or similar nature'. Turkey was not competing that year and its Eurovision broadcaster TRT decided at the last minute not to show the contest, although it denied that the decision was connected to the prospect of a lesbian kiss. It was just coincidence, it said. China did screen a pre-recorded version of the contest but edited out the sensational snog.

Benjamin Cohen, publisher of PinkNews, had said before the contest: 'Eurovision is often referred to as "the gay World Cup" thanks to its camp celebration of popular culture and the fact that so many gay people tune in. So a song that appeals to gay voters is a particularly clever idea.' Unfortunately for Siegfrids, who even lobbed a few Eurovision-friendly 'ding dongs' into the song, most of that year's voters must have been homophobic because Finland only picked up thirteen votes.

WEREWOLVES AND DRACULA (2013)

One song that Eurovision audiences were sadly deprived of in 2013 was '*Meiecundimees Üks Korsakov Läks Eile Lätti*' ('A Local Man Korsakov went to Latvia Yesterday') by Estonian punk metal band Winny Puhh. I'm sure you won't need reminding of their classic 2006 track '*Nuudlid Ja Hapupiim*' ('Noodles and Sour Milk'). The Eurovision Song Contest might have seemed an unlikely route for such a band to take but, after Lordi, anything goes.

For the Estonian selection show, Winny Puhh dressed as were-wolves, wore metallic wrestling costumes and hammered out their song, which basically consisted of the singer repeating the title thirty-one times in a frantic, high-pitched voice. The two drummers started off hanging upside down and by the end the guitarists were also suspended upside down in mid-air. Despite their extravagant stage show, they finished third, and instead Estonia chose a nice singer, Birgit Õigemeel, who could safely be allowed out when there was a full moon.

Every bit as eccentric was Romania's Cezar who dressed worry-ingly like Dracula to perform 'It's My Life'. He sang throughout in falsetto – the first finalist in the history of the competition to do so – possibly as a result of having sat on a stake. Part-way through his performance, he appeared to levitate, presumably so that he could hit even higher notes. The whole thing was gloriously over-the-top. He was sufficiently different to impress a number of voters and finished thirteenth in the final on sixty-five points, including tens from Moldova (no surprise there) and Greece.

THE BEARDED LADY (2014)

The 2014 contest in Copenhagen was all about one person, Austria's Conchita Wurst or, as Google Translate calls her, Conchita Sausage. Of course, she was not the first drag act to appear at Eurovision – or even to win it – but she was the first drag act with a beard. It made her a photographer's dream and a Neanderthal's nightmare.

She is the alter ego of Tom Neuwirth who used to be a member of an Austrian boy band, Jetzt Anders!, before developing her persona in 2011. He revealed that he took the name Conchita from a Cuban friend and that '*wurst*' is part of a German expression for 'it's all the same to me' and 'I don't care'. That was an image that he wanted to put across, although he subsequently discovered that '*conchita*' is also Spanish slang for 'vagina' and that '*wurst*' is German slang for 'penis'. He said the inclusion of Conchita's dark beard was 'a statement to say that you can achieve anything, no matter who you are or how you look. People only look at my beard for a moment, then it melts away and it's just another part of me. It's the most natural thing – this is what a bearded lady looks like. There's a big difference between when I'm Tom and when I'm Conchita. Conchita uses very proper German; Tom talks in an Austrian dialect. Conchita gets mad if she is kept waiting; Tom is lazy.'

Sensing that Eurovision was her spiritual home, Conchita first tried out for the contest in 2012 but finished runner-up in the Austrian national final behind the dreadful Trackshittaz. Fortunately, her time would come, and she was picked to represent her country in 2014 with the song 'Rise Like A Phoenix'. Her selection sparked outrage in parts of eastern Europe. Petitions in Russia and Belarus called for their respective broadcasters to edit out Wurst's performance, the Russian petition stating that the Eurovision had become a 'hotbed of sodomy at the initiation of European liberals'. Russian politician Vitaly Milonov waded into the row by urging Russia to boycott the competition, saying Wurst represented 'blatant propaganda of homosexuality and spiritual decay' and referring to her as the 'pervert from Austria'. So she probably wasn't expecting many points from Russia, although in the end she picked up five. Milonov has their names.

After sweeping to victory with 290 points – Austria's first Eurovision success since 1966 – Wurst returned home, where she was greeted at Vienna airport by more than a thousand cheering fans, many wearing fake beards and singing 'Rise Like A Phoenix'. The Austrian president declared it to be 'not just a victory for Austria but above all for diversity and tolerance in Europe'. A local radio station celebrated by playing the song on a loop forty-eight times over four hours. This tactic of playing the same Eurovision song over and over again for hours not only appealed to diehard fans but also to national security agencies on the lookout for new methods of mental torture. If Henry V had played 'Save Your Kisses For Me' non-stop for four hours at Agincourt, the French would have quickly surrendered.

At the 2014 Eurovision, Molly Smitten-Downes finished a distant seventeenth for the UK with her song 'Children of the Universe'. What she lacked was a powerful message, a campaign, and a beard.

THE FIRST EUROVISION MP (2014)

Not only did 2014 mark the first bearded lady to win Eurovision, it was also the first year that a serving MP sang in the contest. Óttarr Proppé, a politician with Iceland's Bright Future party and the member of parliament for Reykjavik South, was one of the backing singers for band Pollapönk as they performed '*Enga Fordóma*' ('No Prejudice').

Sporting a purple suit, sunglasses and a beard that ZZ Top would be proud of, let alone Conchita, Proppé looked anything but a politician. He was not simply plucked out of thin air as a political gimmick – he has performed with a number of Icelandic rock and punk bands and has even appeared in a couple of films. It is perhaps just as well that Iceland finished no higher than fifteenth in the final because, as a change from kissing babies, other countries' vote-hungry politicians might have been tempted to seek popularity and publicity by taking part in future Eurovisions. Is that Angela Merkel on drums and Iain Duncan Smith on the double-necked axe?

BANISHING THE
WASHDAY BLUES (2014)

Facial hair was a recurring theme in 2014 as the French entry, 'Moustache' by Twin Twin, told how for all the singer's wealth, flash car and trendy clothes, what he really wanted more than anything else in the world was to grow a moustache. It didn't deserve to finish last in the final, picking up just two points, but a record of just one Top 10 finish since 2002 suggests that the French are almost as unpopular with the rest of Europe as the British.

Russia's Tolmachevy Sisters (twins Anastasiya and Maria) began their performance of 'Shine' standing side by side with their long hair tied together. Scottish football fans never expected to see Ayr United at the Eurovision Song Contest. Fortunately it was joined loosely enough to allow them to go their separate ways after a few bars, thus avoiding an unsightly pile-up on stage.

No expense was spared in the presentations with Ukraine featuring a backing singer in a hamster wheel, the Azerbaijan singer performing alongside a trapeze artist, and Poland's Donatan & Cleo going for raw sex appeal. Their song, '*My Słowianie*' ('We Are Slavic'), referred to the local girls' 'hot Slavic blood' and their performance featured a buxom young washer-woman who threatened to do for washing clothes what *Ghost* did for pottery. This was no mean feat because, as has been well documented, front-loaders aren't always the most popular at Eurovision.

GEORGIA'S HOPES
GO UP IN SMOKE (2015)

Two songs titled 'Warrior' entered Eurovision 2015, but, with Malta's failing to pick up enough votes in the semi-final, only Georgia's Nina Sublatti reached the final. There, the black-clad, sultry fantasy heroine found herself facing an unexpected enemy – a malfunctioning smoke machine.

In the semi-final, the machine had spewed out just the right amount of smoke to create the required air of mystery but here it went into overdrive, creating a scene reminiscent of one of those infamous London pea-souper smogs of the 1950s. Thick grey clouds of smoke belched out across the stage at such height and density that poor Nina disappeared from view altogether before the first chorus. She re-emerged periodically but it would have not surprised some of the more elderly audience members in Vienna had she done so wearing a gas mask, which is rarely a good look, even at Eurovision.

The machine did eventually behave in a more restrained manner, enabling Nina to remain in vision for the second half of the song and the warrior battled on bravely. However, her fans were not happy and let their feelings be known in online forums. She ended up down in eleventh place despite being one of the pre-contest favourites. It seems her hopes had gone up in smoke. Coincidentally, the German entry was titled 'Black Smoke'.

VOTING SENSATION
ROCKS EUROVISION (2015)

Australia joined the Eurovision party in 2015 which, if nothing else, silenced those who had always protested that Israel wasn't part of Europe. Australia has broadcast the contest for over thirty years and the event has acquired a cult following there, so the Aussies happily accepted when the EBU invited them to participate in the sixtieth edition of Eurovision. Their presence was in keeping with that year's Eurovision theme of 'building bridges', although it would take one hell of a bridge to stretch from Paris to Sydney.

To make Australia feel that it was becoming a member of one big happy family, who never, ever, ever fell out, the Lithuanian entry featured an unprecedented double gay kiss and anti-booing technology was installed with the intention of suppressing the vocal ill-feeling that had manifested itself in recent years whenever anyone voted for Russia. The hostility towards Russia was widely attributed to its controversial military action in Ukraine and its uncompromising stance on homosexuality. Although the mysterious sound reducers were meant to stop the jeers from being broadcast, the Russian singer, Polina Gagarina, appeared to be crying in the green room during the voting procedure, reportedly as a result of the booing. Given the length of time the voting takes and the number of votes Russia received (303) she must have shed a lot of tears. She eventually finished second behind Sweden, with Australia's Guy Sebastian back in fifth.

But these were just minor stories next to the major shock of the night, puffs of wind before the tornado, small tremors before the earthquake. For the 2015 Eurovision produced a sensation of seismic proportions. Just as people traditionally exchange presents at Christmas, Greece and Cyprus traditionally exchange *douze points* at Eurovision; but in 2015 all that bonhomie suddenly vanished when Greece only gave Cyprus ten and Cyprus awarded Greece a measly eight points. To put this into context, the last time Greece had given Cyprus fewer than twelve points was 1995 (eight) and the last time Cyprus had given Greece fewer than twelve was 1996 (ten). Front pages were being held across the world; seasoned Eurovision observers were left reeling.

Cypriot TV voters had actually ranked the Greek singer, Maria-Elena Kyriakou, in first place, which was no more than expected, especially as she hails from the island. However, the Cypriot jury placed her song 'One Last Breath' only sixth, resulting in Greece receiving just eight points. 'It was terribly unfair,' wailed Maria-Elena. 'I got really upset. I was having fun, but then the voting procedure began, and I was in shock. I felt embarrassed after hearing the Cypriot vote. I did not expect such a thing from Cyprus. Only five people [the jury] decided this horrific result.' It was hard not to feel some sympathy for her, that after such a prolonged mutual love-in, she had to be the one to find out that Cyprus was sleeping with another country. The matter was deemed so grave that it was discussed between politicians from

Greece and Cyprus. Well, it's not as if Greek politicians have anything more important to worry about.

It is comforting to know that even after sixty years, the Eurovision Song Contest still has the capacity to leave us open-mouthed in amazement.

APPENDIX I

EUROVISION WINNERS
1956 Switzerland, Lys Assia, 'Refrain'
1957 Netherlands, Corry Brokken, '*Net Als Toen*'
1958 France, André Claveau, '*Dors, Mon Amour*'
1959 Netherlands, Teddy Scholten, '*Een Beetje*'
1960 France, Jacqueline Boyer, '*Tom Pillibi*'
1961 Luxembourg, Jean-Claude Pascal, '*Nous Les Amoureux*'
1962 France, Isabelle Aubret, '*Un Premier Amour*'
1963 Denmark, Grethe and Jørgen Ingmann, '*Dansevise*'
1964 Italy, Gigliola Cinquetti, '*Non Ho L'Eta*'
1965 Luxembourg, France Gall, '*Poupée De Cire, Poupée De Son*'
1966 Austria, Udo Jürgens, '*Merci Chérie*'
1967 United Kingdom, Sandie Shaw, 'Puppet on a String'
1968 Spain, Massiel, 'La La La'
1969 Spain, Salomé, '*Vivo Cantando*'
    United Kingdom, Lulu, 'Boom Bang-A-Bang'
    Netherlands, Lenny Kuhr, '*De Troubadour*'
    France, Frida Boccara, '*Un Jour, Un Enfant*'
1970 Ireland, Dana, 'All Kinds of Everything'
1971 Monaco, Séverine, '*Un Banc, Un Arbre, Une Rue*'
1972 Luxembourg, Vicky Leandros, '*Après Toi*'

1973 Luxembourg, Anne-Marie David, *'Tu Tu Reconnaîtras'*

1974 Sweden, ABBA, 'Waterloo'

1975 Netherlands, Teach-In, 'Ding Dinge Dong'

1976 United Kingdom, Brotherhood Of Man, 'Save Your Kisses For Me'

1977 France, Marie Myriam, *'L'Oiseau Et L'Enfant'*

1978 Israel, Izhar Cohen and Alphabeta, 'A-Ba-Ni-Bi'

1979 Israel, Milk and Honey, 'Hallelujah'

1980 Ireland, Johnny Logan, 'What's Another Year?'

1981 United Kingdom, Bucks Fizz, 'Making Your Mind Up'

1982 Germany, Nicole, *'Ein Bisschen Frieden'*

1983 Luxembourg, Corinne Hermès, *'Si La Vie Est Cadeau'*

1984 Sweden, Herreys, 'Diggi-Loo Diggi-Ley'

1985 Norway, Bobbysocks!, *'La Det Swinge'*

1986 Belgium, Sandra Kim, *'J'ime La Vie'*

1987 Ireland, Johnny Logan, 'Hold Me Now'

1988 Switzerland, Celine Dion, *'Ne Partez Pas Sans Moi'*

1989 Yugoslavia, Riva, 'Rock Me'

1990 Italy, Toto Cutugno, *'Insieme: 1992'*

1991 Sweden, Carola, *'Fångad Av En Stormvind'*

1992 Ireland, Linda Martin, 'Why Me?'

1993 Ireland, Niamh Kavanagh, 'In Your Eyes'

1994 Ireland, Paul Harrington with Charlie McGettigan, 'Rock 'n' Roll Kids'

1995 Norway, Secret Garden, 'Nocturne'

1996 Ireland, Eimear Quinn, 'The Voice'

1997 United Kingdom, Katrina and the Waves, 'Love Shine A Light'

1998 Israel, Dana International, 'Diva'

1999 Sweden, Charlotte Nilsson, 'Take Me To Your Heaven'
2000 Denmark, Olsen Brothers, 'Fly On The Wings of Love'
2001 Estonia, Tanel Padar, Dave Benton and 2XL, 'Everybody'
2002 Latvia, Marie N, 'I Wanna'
2003 Turkey, Sertab Erener, 'Every Way That I Can'
2004 Ukraine, Ruslana, 'Wild Dances'
2005 Greece, Helena Paparizou, 'My Number One'
2006 Finland, Lordi, 'Hard Rock Hallelujah'
2007 Serbia, Marija Šerifović, *Molitva*
2008 Russia, Dima Bilan, 'Believe'
2009 Norway, Alexander Rybak, 'Fairy tale'
2010 Germany, Lena, 'Satellite'
2011 Azerbaijan, Ell & Nikki, 'Running Scared'
2012 Sweden, Loreen, 'Euphoria'
2013 Denmark, Emmelie de Forest, 'Only Teardrops'
2014 Austria, Conchita Wurst, 'Rise Like A Phoenix'
2015 Sweden, Måns Zelmerlöw, 'Heroes'

APPENDIX II

NUL POINTERS

1962 Belgium, Fud Leclerc, '*Ton Nom*'
Spain, Victor Balaguer, '*Llámame*'
Austria, Eleonore Schwarz, '*Nur In Der Wiener Luft*'
Netherlands, De Spelbrekers, '*Katinka*'
1963 Netherlands, Annie Palmen, '*Een Speeldoos*'
Norway, Anita Thallaug, '*Solhverv*'
Finland, Laila Halme, '*Muistojeni Laulu*'
Sweden, Monica Zetterlund, '*En Gång i Stockholm*'
1964 Portugal, António Calvario, '*Oração*'
Germany, Nora Nova, '*Man Gewöhnt Sich so Schnell an das Schöne*'
Yugoslavia, Sabahudin Kurt, '*Život Je Sklopio Krug*'
Switzerland, Anita Traversi, '*I Miei Pensieri*'
1965 Spain, Conchita Bautista, '*Que Bueno, Que Bueno*'
Germany, Ulla Wiesner, '*Paradies, Wo Bist Du?*'
Belgium, Lize Marke, '*Als Het Weer Lente Is*'
Finland, Viktor Klimenko, '*Aurinko Laskee Lånteen*'
1966 Monaco, Tereza, '*Bien Plus Fort*'
Italy, Domenico Modugno, '*Dio, Come Ti Amo*'
1967 Switzerland, Géraldine, '*Quel Coeur Vas-tu Briser?*'

1970 Luxembourg, David Alexandre Winter, '*Je Suis Tombé du Ciel*'

1978 Norway, Jahn Teigen, '*Mil Etter Mil*'

1981 Norway, Finn Kalvik, '*Aldri I Livet*'

1982 Finland, Kojo, '*Nuku Pommiin*'

1983 Turkey, Çetin Alp and the Short Waves, 'Opera'

      Spain, Remedios Amaya, '*Quién Maneja Mi Barca?*'

1987 Turkey, Seyyal Taner and Locomotif, '*Şarkım Sevgi Üstüne*'

1988 Austria, Wilfried, 'Lisa, Mona Lisa'

1989 Iceland, Daníel Ágúst Haraldsson, '*Það sem enginn sér*'

1991 Austria, Thomas Forstner, '*Venedig im Regen*'

1994 Lithuania, Ovidijus Vyšniauskas, '*Lopšinė mylimai*'

1997 Norway, Tor Endresen, 'San Francisco'

      Portugal, Celia Lawson, '*Antes Do Adeus*'

1998 Switzerland, Gunvor, '*Lass' Ihn*'

2003 United Kingdom, Jemini, 'Cry Baby'

2015 Austria, The Makemakes, 'I Am Yours'

      Germany, Ann Sophie, 'Black Smoke'

APPENDIX III

1976 Brotherhood of Man, 'Save Your Kisses For Me', first
1977 Lynsey de Paul and Mike Moran, 'Rock Bottom', second
1978 Co-Co, 'The Bad Old Days', eleventh
1979 Black Lace, 'Mary Ann', seventh
1980 Prima Donna, 'Love Enough For Two', third
1981 Bucks Fizz, 'Making Your Mind Up', first
1982 Bardo, 'One Step Further', seventh
1983 Sweet Dreams, 'I'm Never Giving Up', sixth
1984 Belle and the Devotions, 'Love Games', seventh
1985 Vikki, 'Love Is', fourth
1986 Ryder, 'Runner In The Night', seventh
1987 Rikki, 'Only The Light', thirteenth
1988 Scott Fitzgerald, 'Go', second
1989 Live Report, 'Why Do I Always Get It Wrong?', second
1990 Emma, 'Give A Little Love Back To The World', sixth
1991 Samantha Janus, 'A Message To Your Heart', tenth
1992 Michael Ball, 'One Step Out Of Time', second
1993 Sonia, 'Better The Devil You Know', second
1994 Frances Ruffelle, 'Lonely Symphony (We Will Be Free)', tenth
1995 Love City Groove, 'Love City Groove', tenth
1996 Gina G, 'Ooh Aah . . . Just A Little Bit', eighth
1997 Katrina and the Waves, 'Love Shine A Light', first
1998 Imaani, 'Where Are You?', second
1999 Precious, 'Say It Again', twelfth
2000 Nicki French, 'Don't Play that Song Again', sixteenth
2001 Lindsay, 'No Dream Impossible', fifteenth
2002 Jessica Garlick, 'Come Back', third
2003 Jemini, 'Cry Baby', twenty-sixth
2004 James Fox, 'Hold On To Our Love', sixteenth

2005 Javine, 'Touch My Fire', twenty-second

2006 Daz Sampson, 'Teenage Life', nineteenth

2007 Scooch, 'Flying The Flag (For You)', twenty-second

2008 Andy Abraham, 'Even If', twenty-fifth

2009 Jade Ewen, 'It's My Time', fifth

2010 Josh Dubovie, 'That Sounds Good To Me', twenty-fifth

2011 Blue, 'I Can', eleventh

2012 Engelbert Humperdinck, 'Love Will Set You Free', twenty-fifth

2013 Bonnie Tyler, 'Believe In Me', nineteenth

2014 Molly, 'Children of the Universe', seventeenth

2015 Electro Velvet, 'Still In Love With You', twenty-fourth

APPENDIX IV

MEMORABLE EUROVISION CLIPS

Here are some of the finest moments from the contest. All links were working perfectly at the time of writing but – in the tradition of Eurovision itself – apologies if you experience any technical difficulties in the broadcast . . .

Denmark (1957) www.youtube.com/watch?v=Q2700K4KY7k
United Kingdom (1959) www.youtube.com/watch?v=-Etl1zYvNSE
Norway (1960) www.youtube.com/watch?v=gvPiePomys4
France (1961) www.youtube.com/watch?v=tUSdvnxfhe4
France (1965) www.youtube.com/watch?v=S6xGnAFFbo8
United Kingdom (1966) www.youtube.com/
   watch?v=SH8BQmfhUgo
Italy (1966) www.youtube.com/watch?v=07KDpfvb2-Y
Spain (1968) www.youtube.com/watch?v=J4g5QYJOFzQ
United Kingdom (1969) www.youtube.com/watch?v=4ew43u2gSoY
Sweden (1973) www.youtube.com/watch?v=hpCgiswUrqQ
Norway (1973) www.youtube.com/watch?v=ITj93XBiZc8
Portugal (1974) www.youtube.com/watch?v=MrW6zP161QI
Netherlands (1975) www.youtube.com/watch?v=5zNVRMabSTU
Greece (1976) www.youtube.com/watch?v=50YT4q7Olcs

Switzerland (1976) www.youtube.com/watch?v=JqlGCtjKzQw
Austria (1977) www.youtube.com/watch?v=yTygxa3p8c4
Norway (1978) www.youtube.com/watch?v=dVj8tlXQ1Vg
Germany (1979) www.youtube.com/watch?v=eAEUrp2V4ss
Switzerland (1979) www.youtube.com/watch?v=pcTCtzsOK18
Greece (1979) www.youtube.com/watch?v=dGg-lbRGWBc
Norway (1980) www.youtube.com/watch?v=piojrkWUmFA
Belgium (1980) www.youtube.com/watch?v=qwDsblonvA8
Finland (1982) www.youtube.com/watch?v=xUoKFwc3U8c
Turkey (1983) www.youtube.com/watch?v=piojrkWUmFA
Sweden (1984) www.youtube.com/watch?v=xvR8C3s9Alo
United Kingdom (1984) www.youtube.com/watch?v=oYIPj5ZuZmA
Israel (1987) www.youtube.com/watch?v=A5nbOUJeQ7s
Turkey (1987) www.youtube.com/watch?v=5F6k4FtDE_Y
Spain (1990) www.youtube.com/watch?v=hNw7Z5Y6xxs
Austria (1991) www.youtube.com/watch?v=uXopu46kMak
Greece (1991) www.youtube.com/watch?v=NjavGxA2aKY
Belgium (1993) www.youtube.com/watch?v=WShutExpu5Y
France (1994) www.youtube.com/watch?v=OxlTRR12EMc
Ireland (1995) www.youtube.com/watch?v=UOnC4CKwioo
Denmark (1997) www.youtube.com/watch?v=rpmYMhzn2iU
Germany (1998) www.youtube.com/watch?v=pJgszpNj7dY
Israel (2000) www.youtube.com/watch?v=3uNfhj66GOo
Slovenia (2002) www.youtube.com/watch?v=lq1MjjZCMQk
Greece (2002) www.youtube.com/watch?v=hiTOVNRS-vw
United Kingdom (2003) www.youtube.com/watch?v=Eu5kgSeZHfw
Belgium (2003) www.youtube.com/watch?v=RRQlsvWMWBo
Austria (2003) www.youtube.com/watch?v=nZJt6Gv4XPk
Switzerland (2004) www.youtube.com/watch?v=EUX3_0KM7fc

Moldova (2005) www.youtube.com/watch?v=RWQCgSB_lpE

Finland (2006) www.youtube.com/watch?v=gAh9NRGNhUU

Lithuania (2006) www.youtube.com/watch?v=o-fAe7SwdqE

Latvia (2006) www.youtube.com/watch?v=cZHsmVinvWY

United Kingdom (2006) www.youtube.com/
watch?v=OYgE7OoOLyw

United Kingdom (2007) www.youtube.com/
watch?v=f9y8hqsYXTw

Ukraine (2007) www.youtube.com/watch?v=3XGMb5PakOQ

Ireland (2008) www.youtube.com/watch?v=-n–JnAwirk

Latvia (2008) www.youtube.com/watch?v=zHLqfkU_oxA

Azerbaijan (2008) www.youtube.com/watch?v=eooVrY5C-ow

Lithuania (2010) www.youtube.com/watch?v=ko_Pdbm5B_Y

Moldova (2011) www.youtube.com/watch?v=M3awRSpP3WY

Russia (2012) www.youtube.com/watch?v=BgUstrmJzyc

San Marino (2012) www.youtube.com/watch?v=y7loR_5HPQo

Austria (2012) www.youtube.com/watch?v=BKQf8Z5uWQ8

Finland (2013) www.youtube.com/watch?v=dlBXOveVh7c

Estonia (2013) www.youtube.com/watch?v=TjN3P2idpol

Romania (2013) www.youtube.com/watch?v= b5KinC75chM

Poland (2014) www.youtube.com/watch?v=q8J3GAg5zal

Georgia (2015) www.youtube.com/watch?v=ddC8lviTERI

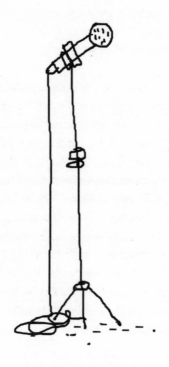

Crap Kitchen

Geoff Tibballs

Available to buy in ebook and paperback

The worst cookbook ever, packed with truly bizarre and utterly disgusting recipes from all over the world.

Ever since humankind produced its first foodie, the culinary world has dished up some staggering confections which could best be described as 'acquired tastes': dishes such as virgin boy eggs (eggs soaked in the urine of prepubescent boys); calf-brain custard; and beard beer, made from the yeast found in facial hair.

From the Roman Empire (grilled cow's womb) to modern-day China (tuna eyeball) via Sardinia (maggot-infested cheese) and Vietnam (the still-beating heart of a snake), this is the most revolting cookbook you'll ever read. Bon appétit!

The World's 100 Weirdest Museums

Geoff Tibballs

Available to buy in ebook and paperback

A guide to the weirdest and most wonderful museums in the world, from the Currywurst Museum of Berlin to the Kansas Barbed Wire Museum.

When we think of the world's great museums, we tend to think of the Louvre, the Guggenheim or the Victoria and Albert. We do not immediately think of the Dog Collar Museum, the Museum of Broken Relationships or Barney Smith's Toilet Seat Art Museum. Yet scattered across the globe are museums dedicated to every conceivable subject, from bananas to Bigfoot, lawn-mowers to leprechauns, teapots to tapeworms, mustard to moist towelettes, and pencils to penises.

Each entry includes address, contact and admission details, so the next time you are in the Tennessee mountain resort of Gatlinburg there is no excuse for missing out on a visit the Salt and Pepper Shaker Museum.